THE POWER OF YES PRESENTS:

BUILDING YOUR NETWORK MARKETING BUSINESS
WITHOUT LEAVING YOUR COMFORT ZONE

A collection of stories of personal goals and successes
curated

by Stacey Hall

Building Your Network Marketing Business Without Leaving Your Comfort Zone

Stacey Hall – Executive Producer

Lil Barcaski - Producer

Edited by Linda Hinkle and Lil Barcaski

Published by: GWN Publishing

www.GWNPublishing.com

Cover Design: Kristina Conatser – GFAD Design / LongBar Creative Solutions

www.longbarcreatives.com

ISBN: 978-1-7367932-6-8

CONTENTS

FOREWORD

I've been personally involved in the network marketing profession now for nearly 20 years.

For the last 10+ years, my organization (My Lead System Pro) has served the network marketing industry by directly teaching and training independent distributors how to grow their business using the internet.

I have personally seen how the industry has positively impacted thousands of people I've known over the years.

What I have always loved about the network marketing industry is how it is the ideal vehicle to introduce entrepreneurship to people who've never before started a business yet have the drive and desire to take control of their financial security and their future.

It is a vehicle that breaks down the many barriers to entry that stand in the way of most people being able to start their own business.

For a relatively small financial investment (with such little risk and free of all the typical burdens of traditional business), any individual who has the desire and the drive can get started learning the critical skills required to grow their income as an entrepreneur.

It's little wonder that the network marketing industry continues to experience such tremendous growth, especially in times of economic instability.

We, at MLSP, are very encouraged that a book such as this has been published and sold through major booksellers.

We see it as one more way to inspire, empower, and educate millions of people around the world to explore and consider the network marketing industry as a viable and legitimate option to take control of their paycheck, their financial security, and their future.

Our way at MLSP, is to show entrepreneurs how easy it is to now be able to communicate with thousands of potential prospects all around the world using social media websites.

By learning a few simple skills and techniques, you can build your own global networks of people matching your ideal audience from the comfort of your home, even while working in your pajamas.

The internet has made the dream of a home-based business even more real than ever before.

Sadly, too many people give up on their dreams; too many people, settle for what they have, for what their boss offers them, what the government gives us and what the economy determines.

It is incredibly inspiring to see this book and imagine how many more people may be inspired to take that leap into entrepreneurship, to rediscover their passion and their dreams and to finally be able to make progress towards their financial goals.

The time is ideal for a book like this. Share it with those you love.

— **NORBERT ORLEWICZ**, Co-Founder, My Lead System Pro
https://book.gorforyeschallenge.com

ENDORSEMENTS

"Dreams do come true. Yes, even YOURS. But you have to meet them part way. Get this book as the first step towards them. Read it. Do it. Expect Miracles!"

— **DR. JOE VITALE**, author Zero Limits, one of the stars of the hit movie, "The Secret."
www.VitaleLifeMastery.com

"The Network Marketing industry is by no means new, but thanks to social media & attraction marketing, global opportunities and the level of professionalism, the network marketing business model is one the smartest options to build your financial future and create a legacy for your family.

Stacey Hall, the globally recognized author of books on Attraction Marketing, knows first-hand what it takes to build a successful network marketing business online and off. This time, she has brought together some of the leaders in our profession, each one with a story that will make you stop and think, 'Is this for me? Should I explore my options further? What is my Plan B?'

Don't ignore that intuitive voice. This book is all you need to join forces with a supportive community of entrepreneurs who are changing the world by helping others improve their lives."

— **JACKIE SHARPE**, Empowering Entrepreneurs and Network Marketers to Create the Life They Truly Deserve
www.EmpoweringEntrepreneursInstitute.com

"The Power of YES series by Stacey Hall is a brilliant compilation of stories from a strong group of powerful people with a story to tell, that will benefit many. Stacey is the best person to bring together these people to help our profession! Enjoy and learn."

— **GEORGE MADIOU**, Publisher of The Network Marketing Magazine
https://thenetworkmarketingmagazine.com/

"The network marketing industry has been such a blessing! It has allowed me more time and financial freedom than I ever imagined! Not only do I get to create my perfect day EVERY DAY, but I can do it from anywhere in the world! If you are looking to up your skills in network marketing, I am THRILLED for you that you have picked up this book! Do yourself a favor and read it from cover to cover and implement what you learn!"

— **ERIN BIRCH**, Network Marketer, Business and Personal
Transformation Coach and Trainer
erinbirchcoaching.com

"This is a must-read guide for anyone considering Network Marketing. Each author offers thought-provoking tips for creating your dream life."

— **ANTONIO THOMPSON**, Marketing Agency Owner
www.antoniorthompson.com

"The ability to focus amidst the chaos of ongoing life is a vital and essential skill for successful living. Each of the Authors of "The Power of YES…" have created and share how they have prioritized what is most important to them. Their tips for navigating daily challenges can help you do the same and achieve the quality of life you envision and desire."

— **TARA RAYBURN**, Healthy Habits Community Curator
https://healthyhabitscommunity.com

"I love Network Marketing! It's flat out one of the best, low-risk, low-cost ways for the average person to start a business. And the best thing is, you can build your business while still working at your job, so you can still take care of your family while you're learning!"

— **DR. BOB CLARKE**, Online Marketing Specialist
BobandRosemary.com/consistency

"Network marketing can be life changing! I've seen it first-hand and it has directly impacted my own business through our customers. This book can be a powerful tool to make network marketing life-changing for you, too!"

— **HAYLEE CROWLEY**, Owner Whimsy + Wellness
www.whimsyandwellness.com

"Network Marketing is possibly the only profession or system of distribution that I know of, where an individual can leverage lis-tening, passion, love for others, courage of conviction, and a nominal sum of money, to create an unlimited growing residual income and a life of choice and no regrets."

— **RUSS DEVAN**, Success by Design Global, LLC
https://www.successbysdesign.us

"This book is filled with uplifting stories of how network marketing makes it possible to work from the comfort of your home, build life-long relationships, and live your best life on your own terms."

— **JERRY YERKE**, Co-founder / President, Trujivan

"Network Marketing is the most powerful way for the average person to create financial independence and personal freedom."

— **JIM PACKARD**, co-author of The Consistency Chain for Network Marketing
www.consistencychain.com

"When I think of genuine heartfelt leadership, I think of Stacey Hall. She is an incredible trainer in the profession of Network Marketing. She has a proven track record helping people get results using her "Go For YES" formula. Devour every bit of wisdom she has gathered here. You will NOT be disappointed!"

— **MARK HARBERT**, Marketing Expert & Trainer
MarkHarbert.com

YANKED OUT OF MY COMFORT ZONE

By Brook Visser

When I first started network marketing, we were living in Massachusetts having lived in Europe for seven years. I didn't know anyone in the town I lived in, so I thought I could meet some new people and make a little money at the same time.

I was all signed up and anxious to get going when my director said, "Let's get you started! Every time you are waiting in line, just chat with the women next to you and get her name and number."

I almost fell out of my chair. Chat with people I have never met before? No way! I would be completely mortified.

You see, truth be told, I am an introvert, and the idea that I had to chat with strangers horrified me.

I asked her if I could just send messages to women on Facebook. She said, "No, that is not the way we do marketing here."

I actually broke out in a cold sweat.

The way the company worked is that I needed hosts for in-person parties. The more parties I had per week, the more money I could earn. I had zero parties scheduled for that week. How the heck was I going to get one?

I think my director read my mind because she asked me if I wanted to go with her to the mall to get some new leads.

All I could think about are those salesmen in the '70s who would wear a huge jacket and open it to show thousands of stolen watches.

I took a deep breath and said, "Sure."

We wandered through the mall, and I watched our director schmooze up to women and chat them up, saying how beautiful they are. I have no idea what she said next, but she came back with their names and phone numbers.

Okay, I can do this …

I walked into a store, and I don't even remember what they were selling because I was so focused on achieving my goal. I started chatting up the sales lady. We talked about the weather, her kids, schools and then I said, "Great to meet you" and I left.

I couldn't do it. I couldn't even pry out her name and number. My director said not to just chat, but to get to the point and ask for her contact information in the beginning of the conversation.

I never could do that, so I figured doing the Network Marketing thing was not going to work for me. Ever.

Next, I decided to set up a personal rule for myself. Every day, if I didn't have a party planned, I would have to run around the circle on our road. I figured if I had some sort of punishment, maybe I would finally ask them for their name and number.

Nope! That didn't work either.

What I did do was resign from the company because I figured Network Marketing wasn't going to work for me. Well, I kept stumbling because I really wanted to work from home and have the freedom associated with that lifestyle. I got a coach who could train me to do more online, and I followed many successful network marketers and actually copied what they were doing.

Over the years, I discovered more about who I am and how to express myself. I discovered that Network Marketing is not about selling, but about solving problems. I discovered how to find my perfect audience and not look like a billboard. Looking back at my old posts on Facebook, now makes me cringe because the posts sounded like a billboard ad.

After taking many classes and courses, I realized the power of really caring for others and of having absolutely NO agenda. I finally understood that the world is huge and not EVERYONE wants to buy what I am selling.

Now that I am in my comfort zone, I realize that attraction marketing works, and that we have lots of time and patience to get where we want to get to.

Previously, I was in a race with myself, trying desperately to get those parties booked, to sell that item, and to reach the top of that company.

Now I understand the commitment to having continuity, to staying with one company, and to caring deeply for my customers and teammates. I've also learned how important it is to cheer on your friends who are doing the same even if they are in a different company because they are working hard to find that freedom, just like I am.

So, if you are trying to make it happen in the Network Marketing world, here are my tips:

1. Cheer on everyone who is succeeding from getting their first sale to achieving the highest rank. Everyone appreciates applause.

2. Spend an hour or more commenting on Facebook. You have no agenda but to like/love and say something about what they are posting. This will make you much more visible.

3. Have patience, grasshopper. P-A-T-I-E-N-C-E. Know that the more steps you take in the right direction, your success will come. It always does.

4. Surround yourself with like-minded people. People who believe in you. Do NOT get offended if your family, partner, or close friends are skeptical. Just put those blinders on and move toward your goal.

5. Vision yourself already on the stage, in the car, or buying that second house. I don't mean just getting pictures of those things but closing your eyes and notice the feelings

you have when you walk across that stage, climb into the car, or grab the keys to your new house.

6. It is a process. We are all on a journey. Take great care of yourself and give yourself a break when times get rough. Yes, times will get rough. But they will also be amazing. You GOT this!

— **BROOK VISSER**

website: https://www.bookwithbrook.nl/contact

TURNING LOSS INTO GAIN
By Ann M Cook

I'm Ann M. Cook and I want to share my experiences with you. I am a business owner. My husband and I own a commercial cleaning company. We have been in the commercial cleaning business since 2003. I joined a network marketing company shortly after we started our business. I truly believe that network marketing offers the best avenue to get out of the daily work schedule we have set up. With my early experiences in network marketing, I was able to build a small team. With this small team I had some success, but it was nothing to write home about. I wanted to learn how to build an income so that I wouldn't have to work outside my home and could still be my own boss.

I have been involved in numerous network marketing businesses over the years. They all had the same results. I even took training courses that allowed me to become more familiar with building businesses. These trainings were all based on leads and cold calls. This was not in my comfort zone at all! But that is what they teach you do to—call family, call friends, get out of your comfort zone or you won't be successful.

I am a Type A personality, a true go-getter. When I put my mind to something, I get it done! So, making sales isn't an issue for me. Now, building a team and teaching them how to be successful and get sales was a challenge. I tried teaching them the things I had been taught. I also added in the law of attraction and positive mindset. Which is to say what you want, not what you *don't* want. What you speak into the universe is what you will get. Sadly, even that wasn't working.

I got to the point where I was so frustrated about building a team that I just gave up and went back to cleaning. I took 9 years off from any type of network marketing company. So, again I started a cleaning company from scratch. We didn't even have a rag to our name. Here we were working 7 days a week and 12 hours a day. There was no time to spend with my family or friends and definitely no time to enjoy life. We hadn't had a vacation in over 16 yrs. I knew that my body was getting tired of the physical abuse that happens in this industry.

It was time to take a break. I took another chance at another network marketing company because I loved the products. I decided that this time I would go about it in a different way; I simply shared the product. That method was much better for me, and it met with my values and fit my comfort zone in how I wanted to approach sales. It wasn't pushy or salesy but rather it was allowing people to see if the product was helpful to them. My team began to grow, but my people weren't having success. Maybe it was me? I was having success. I was teaching them to do the same things I was doing. There was a difference, though. I was building relationships, long-lasting friendships. I was getting my business in front of people using Facebook and online vendor events. That was the difference!

While still cleaning and building the business, I had an accident that caused us to lose half of our income. It was a blessing in disguise. Most people would have hit rock bottom. I looked at it in a positive way. It allowed us to slow down and for me to continue to work my direct sales business. I am the type of person that is positive and looks at the bright side of things. Everything happens for a reason.

I was realizing that I was living in chaos with my business. I needed something to get myself organized. I was literally losing customers. I found a product that helped me. While using the product for myself, I realized immediately that this was my home. I was able to help people. My business skyrocketed. My team was growing for the first time in my life. Something was still missing. Then, one day in an online vendor event, I met Stacey Hall. I began talking to Stacey. I was definitely in alignment with her. I took her course, "The Go for YES Challenge™." Just in the short time I have been taking this course, things have really opened up for me. I have more people coming to me without me leaving my comfort zone. You don't have to feel like you are pestering family or friends. You don't have to go through a bunch of No's to get to the Yes! I am connecting with people that need my help and what I have to offer them. My business is skyrocketing! I have been promoted three times and re-ranked three times.

All the knowledge that I learned over the years has worked and Stacey's "The Go for YES Challenge ™" fit in with what I was already doing! Taking her course has also taught me so much that I didn't know.

I was in a vendor event, and I saw the company I am with now. I have found my home and my passion. I am able to help people with their chaotic lives.

— **ANN M COOK**
    email: amncook@gmail.com

It is with great sorrow that I must tell you my husband passed away on November, 27th, 2021. He will always be in my heart.

MAKING ALARMS AND TRAFFIC A THING OF THE PAST

By Monica Wanner

The freedom to be able to work from anywhere you choose, and still be productive! Sounds wonderful, and it's what so many people dream of, right?

For me, it's no longer a dream. I am so fortunate that my Network Marketing business is portable and allows me to be able to do just that.

No more employee issues to deal with, no need to ask the boss for time off for an appointment, and no more daily long commutes! As a snowbird now, I can even sleep in 'cause I go to bed later.

Was the decision to leave a career easy? Heck no! But the benefits of marching to my own drum sure outweighed the challenges. Let me take you through one morning when I was an employee...

It's a luxury to have a coffee machine that begins its day before I do. At 5:00 a.m., it sends that sweet aroma to my nose, even before my eyes peel open. But like most people, I hit the 'snooze' button.

After what feels like only six seconds, the second blare of the alarm is a killjoy as I yawn and stretch, swinging my feet over the side of the bed.

Quick shower, no time for makeup, and rushing to pour myself a steaming hot cup of inspiration before launching out the door. Daylight is starting to peek out behind dawn's curtain. But first, a quick sweep of snow off my vehicle. That's my morning stretch—arms reaching across the windshield before sitting on a cold car seat. It's January in Canada—and my first 25 minutes of every workday. As I drive away, I have a feeling that I forgot something.

The commute is "Me Time" as there is not much traffic at 5:30 in the morning. I'm a "Skid School Graduate", so there was no coffee spilled during the 45-minute drive. Growing up in the snowbelt, I'm adept at avoiding ditches on icy roads and can expertly navigate unplowed streets and highways.

The morning march across the staff parking lot to the main doors is not always the same adventure; today it is doused in salt, while yesterday, it was a pond of slush. Last week, it was a sheet of ice that I slid across with the grace of a baby moose taking its first steps on an icy incline. I did not have a happy landing so today my left arm is showcased in a bright green cast. My dental work is completed, and my shoulder is back in its socket!

At my desk I prepare for the day, and organize my schedule before thinking about heading to the ladies' room. But my cell phone startles my concentration—it's Carson, this morning's presenter letting me know he'll be a few minutes late. I disconnect and finish the last few drops of my cold coffee just in time to hear the 8:00 a.m. bell, signaling the official start of the workday. Like Pavlov's dog, I've been conditioned to react to bells and consult schedules. Now its "game on"—time to greet my first group meeting of the day.

With notes in hand and a smile on my face, I begin, "Good morning, everyone and welcome to …." a loud and very audible curse echoes behind me as Lin spills her coffee across the table. Hot liquid spreads to the table's rounded ledge and drips onto the floor. I make a mental note to not lean my hand on the table.

Gwen's cell phone dings, and she is silent for a moment before jumping up and excusing herself. Seconds later, an alarm shrieks when Mike sneaks in through the rear fire exit. I remain calm and force a sheepish smile. The distractions trigger several thoughts that seep their way into the largest part of my brain, the cerebrum (responsible for thinking and reasoning, problem-solving, and emotions) – "Stay calm and keep smiling, you got this, girl.", "Did I take my meds this morning?" and "Is my appointment at the fracture clinic at 2 or at 3 today?". I then remember what I forgot to bring with me this morning—my lunch, comprised of last night's leftovers.

I take a deep breath in, refocus my thoughts, and continue, "In your document, please refer to the chart on page 7…" when Carson makes his late entrance, shuffling papers, followed by an IT technician scurrying in behind him, adjusting his microphone and suddenly, we are all jolted by a loud screeching noise! That's the positive feedback loop that causes the speaker and microphone to rapidly feed each other more and more signal, until the sound system overloads.

Everyone's hands instinctively and simultaneously reach up to block our ears! Oh... and I still need to use the rest room. Really. I do. But there is no bell for that. It's not scheduled. But I did check and yup, my follow-up appointment at the fracture clinic is at 2 p.m.

Ingrid arrives, waves meekly, rolling her eyes in response to the sound system malfunction. As she steps over Lin's coffee puddle, I make a mental note that smell does not travel down like liquid. Smells travel by a process called diffusion, and Lin's coffee spill has diffused her vanilla chai latté into the first three rows.

It's only 8:11 a.m. and I am questioning my choices. Again.

Is this what I want to do? Exhaust myself every day, and spend my weekends to prepare, trying to accommodate others - excusing them for being late, arriving unprepared, or not even showing up? I'm working hard to support someone else's dream, not mine, at the expense of giving up my freedom and my time with family and friends.

Most people have a desire to work from home because it affords them flexibility. I wanted to make my own decisions and fulfill my passion. Not only did I want flexibility so that I could be less busy and more productive and use my time to focus on what I wanted to do, but I also wanted to be away from the ice and snow.

So, a few years ago, I made the leap into the world of Network Marketing where the emphasis is on me to drive my own business. I live my own lifestyle now while marching to the beat of my drum because I can work from anywhere at any time. This is my biggest advantage! I get up and walk the beach or hike a trail with the dog, a family member, or friends. I can leisurely read the paper and enjoy that morning coffee while it's still hot ... and in my favorite mug.

Today, when the machine brews my cup of morning inspiration, I no longer brood about waking up at 5:00 a.m., facing the snow (or ice), or sitting in traffic. I just roll over appreciating that I no longer use the snooze button. I have all this extra time to spend with my family and to invest in me. And best of all, I can learn and grow so that I am better able to serve others, at my pace.

While there are still some growing pains, I have embraced the new pace of my life. And best of all, I have observed how true entrepreneurs pivot and handle changes, setbacks, and experienced growth.

Are you ready to live your dream, maybe even just part-time? Or will you continue to make someone else's dream come to life? Let's have a hot coffee and chat about this, okay?

— **MONICA WANNER**
email: monica_wanner@yahoo.ca

BLOOM WITHOUT BOUNDARIES

By Effie Y. Sanford

My true nature, once upon a time, was shyness and being extremely introverted. I thought that sales would help me break out of my comfort zone and that meeting new people would help me overcome that shyness. I first got started in sales in the mid-nineties before everything revolved around social media. I soon realized I could not be the pushy saleslady, a busy cold caller, or a walking advertisement so I could schedule 10 or more parties a week. That just wasn't me but, you know, I kept joining companies that expected me to do those same exact things to accrue points and rewards while collecting a percentage of my sales. Some people thrive in that atmosphere. Some, like me, do not. Maybe it is because they have to step out of their comfort zone too often.

Some might say that I was destined to fail. I disagree! I just hadn't found my home ... YET! The various work-from-home jobs didn't hold me for long and for a little while, I would forget that I had an entrepreneurial spirit, and I would stick to "the day job." However, there was always this question that would pop back in my mind, "What was out there for me?" I knew I was made for something very different. I was willing to keep searching until I found what that "different" thing was.

Fast forward to 2015. By this time, I had undertaken many home sales side hustles. This did get me out of my shyness, yet I will always be an introvert at heart. Though these ventures helped my soul growth, it didn't help my finances much. I found out that during several of these ventures I was spending more than I was making, and since I was now a single mom, I had to do something. I had to figure this out!

Hello social media! I was well into social media for almost 15 years by now. I decided to take a leap. I learned to code, and I even built my own website. I was ready to go full throttle into affiliate marketing! And I did. I learned a lot, yet I also learned that I had no idea how to drive traffic or how to do a lot of things that were important in making it all work out. I also had no family or friend support. I was overwhelmed and tired. I'd been going to school and then working on my business during my free time. I eventually took the easy way out and let my site go. I just knew there had to be a better way, and I needed someone to show me how it all worked, but for now, I was going to have to slow down, think, and start over.

Fortunately, I happen to be one of those people that retreats just long enough to regroup and then I step back into the battle once again! I have always believed that nothing is impossible and there is always a way to bring something into fruition if you believe in it and yourself enough. God had given me that little mustard seed of faith, and I was going to use every ounce!

I wanted to work from home, and I wanted to produce a full-time income! I loved the idea of firing my boss, the flexible lifestyle, and having daily options of what I did with my time. I love people, and I love helping them, whether with my products, service or welcoming them as partners. I wanted to help people, mainly women, realize their potential and help transform like a butterfly or rise like the phoenix. Once a person realizes what is inside of them and knows how to use it and let their soul shine, nothing is impossible, and transformation is inevitable!

Lo and behold, 2020 came along and I decided to give network marketing another try and after learning about a couple of well-known companies, I got the bug! I was hooked! I found a place where everybody knows my name, everyone is willing to support and help you, and they aren't pushing you to move out of your comfort zone. They, my teammates and newfound friends, work with me to find what best works for me and how I can tweak things, like making videos. I am now excited every day! Even when I don't feel like it, I get up and I show up because I know that consistency is paramount.

When you find a space that fits your personality and helps you stretch and flex instead of busting out of your own personality and becoming someone else just to make a buck, you stick to it longer, you grow instead of burning out, and you stay you, just better!

I am now home. I get to stay in my comfort zone and just move it this way or that. I've learned to use my creative side to tackle any issues. I'm able to be me and stick with my core values while delivering quality and substance to my customers. I am able to use my story and my new journey to inspire and encourage others just like me.

It's not just about making profits and building your business; it's about sharing yourself with others and helping them along the way. Whether it be the journey, the products I promote, or the fact that I don't have to fully step out of my comfort zone, I now can show others how they can reach their full potential and rise like a phoenix into their own light and bloom without boundaries!

— **EFFIE Y. SANFORD**
email: Effiewrites71@gmail.com

A SURPRISE CATALYST FOR FREEDOM TO REVEL IN MY COMFORT ZONE

By Elaine Payne

Freedom is a concept as well as a reality of choice. Freedom is a value I cherish. My father, who fought in World War II, is my first example of the importance of freedom. His stories, his beliefs, and his actions exemplify the importance of freedom to a life full of possibilities. Freedom for me today is the opportunity to choose: to choose what I say and what I do as I pursue success and happiness in life.

Before getting into network marketing, I was a nurse. I loved nursing; however, there were numerous timed tasks, time constraints, policies, and documentation requirements. There were not many freedom choices. Sleep was difficult. Nutrition equated to grabbing a bite of whatever whenever I could. Values were patient focused. After I retired, a nurse friend introduced me to this business of network marketing.

Freedom in network marketing has opened a variety of doors: choosing the right company; choosing knowledgeable, respected leaders; and choosing products that I value. Ultimately, there is the choice to share a business and products that make my life better, just as I would share a favorite recipe or a wonderful book with a friend.

Network marketing offers creative opportunities that I had not imagined. Social network marketing has been a new knowledge base that I have thoroughly enjoyed learning. This knowledge base has introduced me to remarkable, fun, intelligent, and visionary people from around the world. The current healthcare environment has limited social interaction. Network marketing has allowed relationships to form, grow, and often develop into friendships.

This business continues to open new areas for growth. Meeting other network marketers and seeing the ideas they share on Facebook, LinkedIn, and Instagram offers different and limitless interests, entertainment, and self-fulfillment. Prior to network marketing, my comfort zone certainly did not include writing content, making videos, taking master classes, and meeting masterminds from around the world. I am now a published author because of this opportunity.

A major benefit of network marketing is the freedom to "work" in my comfort zone. My comfort zone is my home, my family, and our three dogs, as well as traveling to places I desire. I take network marketing with me wherever I go. There are no set hours, no set schedule, no set nor limited vacation time, and especially, no traveling to work on snow days! I love the snow, and in my healthcare career, we had to be at the hospital. Snow with a travel advisory was not an excuse. We could go to the hospital when snow was predicted and stay until it was gone, which sometimes meant days!

This business allows me to honor my values, be who I am, and define my own time constraints. My chosen business is in sync and alignment with my priorities in life. In addition, the work aspect is efficient and streamlined to make it easy for busy people to participate. The company's values include a healthy focus with exceptional products that help people.

A "Golden Rule" leadership model is an important reason I align with this business. The leaders are consistent in showing up as support every day. There is education, guidance, and daily communication. I can message the leaders in my company at any time. And I do! They reliably respond and answer any questions. Daily, non-mandatory, open zoom meetings are held for associates to invite potential clients. This flexibility fits my life needs.

This company has an active, supportive community. The business is growing; however, leadership has set standards that maintain mutual respect and support as the business has grown. This growth has not stymied efficiency, nor affected relationships and benefits of the supportive community.

Small successes are celebrated just like the big ones! Humor, which I value more and more each day, is often part of these celebrations. Leaders are happy and positive. Stories are often funny, in addition to sobering testimonies by associates. It is not uncommon for the president of the company to hop in on a zoom, surprising everyone.

A spiritual value expressed in this community is prayer. There are prayer calls one to two times a week. Anyone can participate, and all prayer requests are addressed. I appreciate these gatherings as my spirituality is met with openness and tolerance. The calls are led by leaders and associates. Prayer times help people connect, form meaningful relationships, and promote community.

As an individual, and as a nurse, I view people as biological, psychological, sociological, and spiritual beings. To deny any of these aspects of my life would not be authentic. It would not be true nor right. I am somewhat surprised when I realize that my choice of a network marketing company is a positive contributor to each of these vital aspects.

Biologically, the business is not a stressor. I serve my basic priorities. I sleep better, get more rest, and have "clean" nutrition. I feel good, in part due to the amazing products I support.

Psychologically, my interactions with this community and the persons with whom I choose to partner are positive and emotionally supportive. My mindset is one of optimism and gratitude.

Socially, I am welcomed and supported by a group of fellow entrepreneurs. The texts, zooms, and messages from upline have been helpful, accurate, and address compliance. Such authentic communication assists in a comfort zone for the group.

Spiritually, God is the ultimate priority in my life. I can express this in this business group. I can participate in prayer groups, and I have been invited to share the Prayer of Jabez in the prayer group.

Network marketing has presented me with many opportunities. Numerous doors have opened and continued personal and financial growth is the plan. The value of this business certainly includes financial gain; however, the important gain is that this business allows me to work in my comfort zone while living out my values.

— **ELAINE PAYNE**
   email: Peep1226@gmail.com

COMFORT SCHMOMFORT

By Deb D. Willder

We all love our comfort zones, but as we begin a serious career path, we find out that there can be many opportunities to step outside these spaces of comfort. Grabbing hold of these opportunities can sometimes be a challenge for us and it will mean changing what your comfort zone includes.

After all, if the feeling of comfort signifies our most basic needs being met, why should we seek to abandon it? It's where we feel safe, and we can maintain a steady level of performance with little or no risk.

You may feel perfectly within your comfort zone in a job that you know you are good at, know you can do it with your hands tied behind your back, and that's great if you are genuinely satisfied being there.

Everyone has a different-sized comfort zone. Some will simply sit in the same city, in the same house, doing the same job and they are perfectly happy with their lot.

It's all fine, so long as you are content with where you sit but what if you want more?

Some people want to stretch themselves a little and if they are great at their jobs, head-hunters will find them and seek them out to offer them an even better job for more money. Sometimes they accept this new job and create a new comfort zone expanding a little step by step. Perhaps they will venture further and further, grow bigger and bigger, and their comfort zone will get so expansive that it reaches its limit.

It can be likened to a bubble, and you can push it in different directions and expand it until these objectives of yours—that seem totally crazy—will eventually fall within the realms of the possible.

Well, I am here to tell you that you can have more and stay slap bang in the middle of your zone and have success.

The network marketing industry is made up of businesses that suit people of all shapes, sizes, ages, nationalities, and personalities. It allows mums, dads, grandmas, and grandpas, singles, married people to make money without having to leave the safety of their homes or their personal comfort zones. If you need to build this new career slowly, you don't necessarily need to step out of the comfort zone you've built yet while building your new business and your new comfort zone. You can still have some amazing success and make money.

It's important to choose a network marketing company that means more to you than just a paycheck. If you base your choice on a company that has an amazing compensation plan, though you don't believe in or like the products, because you think it will make you the most money you may find yourself very UNcomfortable. I made that mistake and attempted to create a business though I didn't like the main product. I didn't succeed.

Instead, choose a business you align with that also aligns with your values and that of your family and loved ones. That alignment is also part of your comfort zone.

You must also be willing, if you are to do this Network Marketing thing, to put yourself out a wee bit from your current safe life to let people know what you are doing. If you rely on friends and family to build your new business, that can limit your opportunities. However, if you are willing to stretch yourself and use the internet to your advantage, then the sky can be the limit.

Network marketing is an incredible way to meet new people, even if not in person, because technology allows us to participate in zoom calls where we can chat and have a dialogue, enjoy conversations, and trainings with team members. This means you can make some amazing friends from all over the world and can expand your horizons without leaving home! Working from home is a big comfort zone parameter for many people. It means making money while taking care of your family or being able to work and create revenue even if you are not comfortable in social situations or business meetings where you must appear in person.

BUT…

If you are willing to step outside that comfortable existence you currently sit in, there are options to build this business you have built, create multiple income streams, and create your own business and brand online. This allows you to create multiple business opportunities. It expands your opportunities and of course the money you can make.

While occupying that comfort zone, it's tempting to do less and feel safe, in control and that the environment is on an even keel. Smooth sailing.

The best sailors, however, are not born in smooth waters. It takes guts and a strong sense of self to go out of one comfort zone to find an even better one. It isn't easy but the gold that is found once you step over the invisible line, is just that… Gold.

May your choices reflect your hopes and not your fears.

I have a huge vision that will require a lot of my time and effort, but it's so important to me and I know my current situation, as an employee, isn't getting it done. I haven't gotten there yet, but my vision and my commitment to getting to a place where I will achieve my dreams is powerful.

If you have unrealized dreams, then perhaps is time to put a toe in the water. I am here to help and help you take that step. It's scary and it's challenging but on the flip side, it's exciting and rewarding.

If you are happy in your current comfort zone, I truly wish you great success and happiness. But, if you want more, if you want to come with me (and the many others) to build a legacy income for your family and build a lifestyle and financial freedom, then go the website, grab your bucket list of amazing things you can do to step up and out, and have fun while building your own business. Let's make you a new and even more comfortable comfort zone!

Reach out if you would like to talk to me.

— **DEB D. WILLDER**
email: apuurrrfectlife@gmail.com
website: http://debdwillderwebinar.com

CREATIVITY, INTEGRITY AND COMPASSION

By Deborah Neary

Growing up in England, I became aware of a personal afflic-tion. It was as if I were unable to grasp fundamental things such as mathematics, grammar, and dates in history. These are skills that we are expected to succeed in; the stuff tests are about. I wasn't, to say the least, a model pupil. I didn't fit in; my goal was to grow up and decide what I wanted to be. I wondered if there was a place where cultures gather around to brainstorm before deciding what's best for the whole community. A culture in which curiosity is valued over rote memorization. This is where I belonged.

At the young age of five, I had a revelation: I have agency, and by shifting how I see and approach the world, I can make magic possible. Although perhaps it wasn't a sophisticated thought pro-cess, there existed a burning desire to achieve something unusual and make a meaningful contribution. There is no end to the road of self-improvement and education. This is one reason I love network marketing.

I cried uncontrollably the first day of kindergarten. I hid in a coatroom and a boy approached me, asking why I was crying when everyone else was having a wonderful time. I will never forget his gentle concern, reaching out his hand to console me. In that mo-ment, I promised myself I would overcome that sense of entrapment. It touched my heart as I experienced compassion from someone so young.

On the first day of elementary school, I was sitting at the front of the class, filled with excitement and anticipation. The teacher asked if we had questions. Being aware of my surroundings, I no-ticed that every wooden table had a hole in the top corner, and I wanted to know why it was there. The teacher responded, "That's not a question!" It now occurs to me what a missed opportunity that was for her. Where were the stories of ink wells and quills? Is it any wonder, that the business I'm building now is all about people feeling heard? What I'm creating fits my core belief that sensitivity and creativity can change lives.

Once out of school, I visited what I like to call the "Misguidance Counselor." My father accompanied me for moral support. In a bilious green room, (appropriate adjectives considering my queasiness), the counselor had a book of job options. I told her I didn't know what I wanted to do or where I could fit in and that I would rather die than work in a factory doing repetitive stuff every day. I needed to be creative and find something meaningful with a sense of purpose.

She looked for a moment and said, "Well, you are in luck. They are looking for packers at the local Ryvita Factory."

My father stood up and said, "Did you hear what my daughter said to you? The one situation she told you would destroy her; the one place she said she knows she does not want to find herself; and that is the only option you can suggest?!" We left without another word. It was a pivotal moment in my life and the first time I had felt thoroughly heard and understood.

I was sure there was a way for me to experience the freedom I craved, and it would be unconventional. In the past, my creativity would drive me to and from jobs, in and out of business opportunities, and at times, into depression. Given that integrity is my core value, it now makes sense why I've had different careers along the way in my pursuit of happiness.

One day, on the beaches of Bournemouth, on the English coast, I was walking with my mum and dad. Dad and I talked about the concept of network marketing. With my finger, I drew circles in the sand radiating out from the center and created a flower. I was the flower, and the circles represented the business model. We got excited! The only way the flower could bloom would be through teamwork, collaboration, and helping others. We discussed how this was the complete opposite to the corporate world which he had struggled with and was recently fired from. The reason? He was "too big for his boots!"

My father was a master of reinventing himself. He was an inspirational person and a true leader. Some of that DNA rubbed off on me. He would be immensely proud of what I am building now.

With creativity at the core of my being, I love the endless possibilities of network marketing. But I've found mostly a pattern of:

"Is this IT?"

"This IS IT!!" and finally...

"This is NOT IT!!".

I gave up on finding a company whose core values fit mine. Failing more than once with a network marketing company creates "evidence" for others around us that it simply doesn't work. Loved ones see failures as something to protect us from. Each time I tried and failed, I learned lessons along the way that were steppingstones leading me to new people. I found that the best way to grow is to make mistakes. Past failures do not preclude future successes.

In my twenties, I came to New York to visit a friend. This was a brave step as I didn't know my host well and New York was a long way away from my English home.

When I landed in the USA, I had a great feeling of expansiveness. When visiting a little farmhouse in Greenwich, I met my husband. My heart and intuition told me this was the man I would marry. This event was a milestone I travelled over three thousand miles to reach. We've now been married for over 30 years and have two wonderful children.

I am a photographer; it appeals to my sense of creativity. Although I love to make others happy with the results of beautiful images, I also want to find a way to help beyond that.

Network marketing was always on the backburner. However, I've never forgotten the magic in the sand and the concept of helping others to achieve greatness and in return, creating residual income for everyone, including my own family. This strong intuition made it difficult for me to just let network marketing go. My family had some concerns about me spending so much time and energy on trying to build various networks. After a while, I gave up on the dream.

My husband is practical and logical, and his grounding energy is valuable. Often my head can be in the clouds with magical thinking pipe dreams. This, combined with my family's concern about the business model, became an issue for me and I started to doubt my ability to pull it off. I couldn't argue with them because I feared they were right. The truth is that I loved the idea, but the way my brain works, I couldn't see the forest for the trees. Yet I wanted so badly to explore the idea of residual income and compounding growth. I spent some time re-evaluating my life's purpose and what it was about the multilevel marketing profession that I so loved.

I decided to give in.

I got myself a job and became despondent. Being a wife and mom, I didn't want anyone to notice what I was going through. I thought I could handle it on my own and no one else would be affected.

After years of concealed depression, my 19-year-old daughter came to me and asked if we could talk. I was shocked and filled with admiration for her compassion and bravery. She expressed her concerns that she could no longer spend time with me and wanted me to understand that it was because of how I was being. Ever so gently, with tears and hugs, she asked me to find help. To this day, I am deeply grateful for her honesty, as she opened a door of possibilities, inviting me to walk through it and find a solution.

I found one.

A friend introduced me to a mental wellness company which makes use of the multilevel model for their marketing and distribution. After taking just a few products for one week, my doom and gloom lifted, and then disappeared altogether. Furthermore, in checking out the people who created this company and products, I found that they resonated with my core beliefs. My devoted friend and first wellness partner took me to the company headquarters for their open house. My values, to my utter delight, were literally etched on the glass walls in the main office:

LOVE

INTEGRITY

INNOVATION

SERVICE

HUMILITY

We heard the founders, CEO, and Chief Science Officer, who creates the life-changing products, speak. The timing was perfect, as the products allowed me to see clearly. At last, I'd found a company that promised to fulfill my dream to build a team. This company has attracted so many heart-based leaders and mentors, I am grateful to each one of the people who have dedicated their lives to helping us achieve our goals in life and change the world one person at a time.

Magically, through my art, I found a mentor and business partner who has become a good friend. Over many years I worked on a painting, a catharsis, and had finalized it by writing the Ho'oponopono prayer. After I posted it on Facebook, he reached out to me with an interest to purchase it. He has created a unique perspective on how network marketing can work for people. We have been working together ever since.

Now I can be myself completely and utterly. I love the possibilities network marketing has to offer. Being my authentic self while growing this global community feels like home. I'm in the zone and can push that comfort zone whenever I feel like it. There is no competition -- only cooperation. I found a place where my inner child can play while my intellect can be stimulated.

— **DEBORAH NEARY**
phone: 518 596 8895
email: djdn.photos@gmail.com
website: http://deborahneary.com/

FROM FEAR TO FEAR - LESS

By Donna D. Barron

I remember when I started down the path of creating my own businesses. I had never owned a business before, and I didn't fully understand how to create a business. All I knew was that when I helped others, I felt so fulfilled! It provided my life with even more meaning and purpose. It was so exciting to help someone have an 'Ah Ha!' moment! Every time someone had a breakthrough, or I just helped someone, they were so grateful. Their gratitude gave me the driving force to continue down the path of helping others.

While creating my own online business, I worked with many coaches. One coach wanted me to just jump right out of my comfort zone and do a Facebook live and let the whole world know exactly what I was doing and how I helped others. Looking back now, he had the right idea. However, a little background, I am an introvert who is shy and private. Doing a Facebook live was... well a CRAZY idea for me! I really wanted to stay in my comfort zone, and I felt that would be so out of my comfort zone.

When I joined Facebook, all I did was play games on it. I never posted pictures unless it was a special occasion. I never even commented on other people's posts. When I did attempt to comment on a post, I would analyze the comment, update it, and change it until I would finally delete it and not comment on it at all. It was so frustrating to me. Then I would just disregard the feeling and write it off as I am not a good writer, and no one would want to hear from me anyway. I would just like the post instead, thinking it was just the same and good enough.

Then, an energy healer coach came into my life. I would listen to her healings while I slept. One day, I found myself not just liking a post, I had a comment to write that I liked, and I posted it! I couldn't believe it, and at the same time, I was so excited that I commented on a post. Finally! I finally felt like I was slowly expanding my comfort zone. The best part was they liked my comment and nothing bad happened. It was just a small step in expanding my comfort zone. I finally did it, and if felt great!

While creating my businesses, I was told to network with others by joining various groups. One group I joined was the Facebook Live Challenge group. This group was very engaging. Everyone was doing FB lives. The first challenge was to go live, say your name, where you were from, and what you do. My first thought was, "what did I get myself into?" This was so not what I was expecting. Seriously, I was thinking this was going to be a group where I could get some tips and that would be it. No, it was interactive. The woman who formed the group had stated that it was a safe zone where no one would offer any negative comments, or they would get kicked out of the group. So, I thought, no harm here, I can do this, and what is the worse that's going to happen? My heart was beating fast, and I began staring blankly at the 'go live' button for what seemed like an hour. I finally hit it. I went live! As I did, it dawned on me... this is my very first Live ever. I did it! I thanked this group for helping me expand my comfort zone.

Expanding my comfort zone has been a challenge and yet it has been so thrilling and exhilarating. It slowly led me to expanding my comfort zone even more by posting on my timeline daily and doing Facebook lives. This was huge for me, and once I expanded my comfort zone, baby step, by baby step, I was so relieved. The best part of all is that my posts and Facebook lives are helping others. People have been commenting and letting me know how I have been helping them. I was so afraid of making a mistake and thinking that everyone would laugh at me or pick on me. Now, I have turned that around, and I'm learning that even if I make a mistake, I can use that as content. People like when other people make mistakes. It makes me more relatable. All the things that I feared so much while expanding my comfort zone has turned into something wonderful. As the saying goes 'on the other side of fear is everything that you have ever wanted.' This has been so true for me.

Expanding my comfort zone has led me to an amazing life. I now have my own groups where I help others by offering tips with my posts and Facebook lives. I interviewed one of my coaches and I have many more interviews to come. I have created a free eBook that I offer to anyone who joins my groups with tips that I used in my life that have helped me. I am also in the process of creating a course and a mastermind.

Slowly stretching myself and expanding my comfort zone has also led me to being interviewed on a podcast. It was so much fun that I am thinking about creating a podcast of my own. I also just did my first webinar. To think that all my concerns of expanding my comfort zone and all the fears it brought up that I was able to overcome has turned into something that's been a wonderful experience. It keeps getting better and better every day. I can't wait to see what my future holds as it unfolds while I continue down this path of helping others and creating more and more abundance in my life and the life of others.

— **DONNA D BARRON**
  email: Donnabarron222@gmail.com
  website: https://www.facebook.com/donna.barron.9/
  facebook: https://www.facebook.com/coachdonnadbarron
  instagram: https://instagram.com/donnadbarroncoaching
  youtube: https://www.youtube.com/channel/UCN7fK6dSVdwmX2dETm1To1g

LOVE LIFTED ME
By Darlene Williams

Most Baby Boomers fear they will outlive their income in retirement or will never be able to retire. That was me before Network Marketing made it possible for me to stay in my comfort zone and still earn a good living. It's like having your cake and eating it too.

Words cannot express how wonderful it was to have my son call to ask if I would come help his family when their last child was born. Sometimes I pinch myself as it is almost unbelievable how I can stay in my comfort zone and have such a great life.

I have the freedom to go on vacation for days or weeks at a time, travel the world, or go back and forth to visit my family anytime I want without worrying about hurrying back to punch a clock. I can do so and still have money coming in to take care of my family. I am living life on my terms. It is so wonderful to work from my laptop doing what I want any time I want.

I am not limited to where I work or where I work from. I could be at the pool, on the balcony, on my couch, or wherever I choose. I truly love my life! I can stay in my comfort zone and have fun. A warm fuzzy feeling comes over me every time I think about how blessed I am.

My comfort zone became so comfortable that I actually moved across the country without missing a beat in my business.

I am grateful that I no longer have the glorified babysitting job of working the third shift away from my family all night. It feels great to no longer ask permission to take time off, even to attend the homegoing of a loved one.

Thank goodness I no longer come home and soak my feet or worry about my bones or body hurting from pounding the concrete floors all night. I have done my time at work, that life-bit was rough. I am very glad not to be in that place anymore.

One of the best parts is that I get to go to sleep at night so my body can repair itself. There is no telling how much damage I did to my body staying up all night for 15 years.

After 20 years and 43 days dealing with angry, hostile inmates and listening to their problems and concerns while trying to be fair, there definitely was never a dull moment on my job at the jail. I am so glad I do not have to do that anymore. It also feels good not to have to get in my car late at night to go to work.

Working at a jail in a male-dominated field was no easy task. There is a glass ceiling on any job, especially for women. Not only was my income capped, but there always seemed to be a shortage of female officers. I was truly overworked and underpaid.

The potential for money is considerably greater in Network Marketing. It has provided me with unlimited income potential, and I can make good money without the stress and hustle and bustle of a regular job. If you get it right, the sky is the limit.

I am so grateful that my friend Tim introduced me to my Network Marketing company over 15 years ago. I no longer need to depend on the 40-40-40 plan. If I want to take a week off, I can still work remotely making phone calls and having meetings, all from the comfort of wherever I am.

Honestly, if someone made me show up at a job today, I would make a horrible employee and be truly miserable. I am absolutely unemployable now. I have flashbacks thinking about how I had to take whatever shift and job assignment they gave me, even if it wasn't what I had bid for. There was always the possibility that I could be ordered to work overtime and scramble to find someone to take care of my children until I got off.

Working at a jail, there was never a dull moment as things could always go wrong, a fight could break out at any moment, or someone could get injured. Through it all, I had to remain unbiased.

I also love not being limited to only one place of work and having room to grow in my Network Marketing business. I get to play, explore, and discover endless opportunities without having to be super careful about the things I say or the way I behave for fear of being reprimanded.

Network Marketing allows me to be comfortable doing the things I want to do and the way I want to do them without being forced inside of a box. I am building my own asset, and it's one that I control. Retirement has been such a joy; I don't know how I had time to work.

Network Marketing has allowed me to crack the code, all while being in my comfort zone. I realized that my pension alone would not be enough to take care of my family, especially while my twins were in college. Thanks to having a home-based business, I have been able to correct my W-4P, lower my taxes, eliminate my debt, and build income-producing assets.

I am also breaking the financial curse on my family and leaving an inheritance to my children's children that can be passed on from generation to generation. My grandbabies and great grandbabies will not have to start a job at an entry-level position and work their way up the ladder to retire with each generation repeating the process over and over again.

Now, they will be able to pass the baton of generational wealth from one generation to the next with each generation continuing to build on it.

Millions of people need and desire financial success. You are at the right place at the right time with Network Marketing. Working with me you will get the tools to revamp your personal finances and build your own wealth. Imagine being a debt-free millionaire. The vision has been written and made plain, just follow the GPS to arrive at your personal financial success destination.

— **DARLENE WILLIAMS**
 email: darlene@darlenewilliams.com
 facebook: https://www.facebook.com/groups/tipstomakesureyoudonotout-liveyourincome

SWIMMING IN MY OWN LANE

By Charlice Arnold

My life, before I really dove into network marketing, was considered a dream life to me in many regards. I thought that I had achieved everything I ever wanted or could dream of. I had an amazing man in my life. We traveled the world, had great close friends from all over, had a successful business together, lived in two beautiful homes in Southern California, and had a few fur babies. We loved entertaining, planning our next trips, shopping, exercising, going to live music shows, eating and drinking... On the surface it was amazing!

The major downside however was that the love of my life was dealing with cancer the whole time that we were together. He was diagnosed with colon cancer and had part of it removed right before I met him. He had his ups and downs for the entire time that we knew each other. The treatments were uncomfortable and often caused other health issues for him, yet he never complained and always worked and played hard like he wasn't affected by any of it. This was difficult in many ways, yet being eternal optimists, we were both always positive about the situation. We fully enjoyed every day as much as possible and had many plans for our future together.

Another downside for me was our personal business relationship, which I never shared with anyone. He had been in the swimming pool industry for most of his life. A good friend of ours had been in the plastic molded products business since he was young, and as a freelance bookkeeper for many years, I had the office management, business startup and accounting skills that were necessary to start up and operate a business. We had the idea to utilize all our strengths and connections and start our own business making plastic parts for swimming pools and spas. It took a few years to get the business off the ground, so in the beginning, it was just the three of us doing everything. Then we had a successful boom in sales for the business about five years in when a law got passed that all commercial drains in pools had to be replaced to make them safer so that children didn't get stuck on them and drown. We were one of the first companies to come out with the safer drains that were required per the law. When our business grew exponentially, almost overnight, I hired a staff of office personnel to handle our customer service, admin support, and logistics workload. It was an ever-challenging business expansion, and overall, we enjoyed it very much and were very successful financially.

That all sounds great right? Except the part where I felt disrespected most of the time. I was 15-25 years younger than these two men and always felt like my voice wasn't heard. I would offer my suggestions and continually get told to not talk back and just follow orders when given. I also didn't have a single share in the company even though I was a founder as well as an integral part of its operations. I was treated like an employee instead of a partner in the business that we had all three equally created and helped grow to great success.

When my husband took his last breath and crossed over, I was left dealing with our friend as my partner and only superior at the company. At least I had finally been given a small share of the business as part of my inheritance. However, this partner became increasingly more demanding and less respectful during this time. A few years later, he basically forced me out of the business. Although I don't feel that I got my full value, I received a nice payout for my shares and was then free to figure out what I wanted to do with my future. What did I want to do with this next chapter in my life? I knew that it wasn't sitting behind a desk working for someone else's dreams. I wanted to find something that would be fulfilling to me personally and financially. It was liberating and scary at the same time.

I had a form of PTSD for a while afterwards where I often felt anxiety thinking that I should be doing something for work at every moment, that I wasn't doing enough for my present and future. It was strange to not have to answer to anyone and to not have a full list of tasks that I was supposed to be doing each day. I knew this stemmed from how I had been treated by this past partner and it took me some time to finally take a breath, relax, and focus on myself for once. I began working out and developing better self-care and nutritional habits. I got more into my spiritual practices. I traveled more and spent more time with friends.

It was around that time that I developed some chronic lower back pain. I now know that the root of that pain was not only because I was working out more, but it was also due to the emotional baggage that I was still carrying around related to the grief of the loss of my husband and our business. To find a solution to that pain, I began trying out every alternative remedy and treatment that I could find.

That was when friends of mine introduced me to some products they had been using that could possibly help with my back pain. I felt immediate relief! They asked me if I would host a party for them to help spread the word. I said to myself, I love parties and gathering friends and family and I am loving this product, why not? I had a few people enroll at the event, and then I said to myself, well that was easy, maybe this could be my next venture! So, I dove right in! I wanted to learn everything about doing this business the right way. I knew from past failed network marketing experiences when I was younger that it would take some work, yet this time it was different. I finally felt like I was aligned with a community of people, the lifestyle that it offered, and the mission of the company.

Since then, I have also developed a thriving vacation rental business and positioned myself with a few other network marketing opportunities in wellness and travel that I felt aligned with my core values and that has made all the difference in feeling fulfilled with what I do every day. I enjoy being hospitable, gathering friends, and educating about toxin-free living and healthy habits. I discovered that through network marketing, I can be successful by helping others achieve their wellness goals, their travel bucket lists, and their financial goals while staying true to my own comfort levels. My partners are now my cheerleaders instead of my superiors. I get to work when I want to and not because someone is telling me that I have to. I can do all of my favorite things when I want to... travel, lay out by the pool, spend time with friends and family, live in a beautiful home in a tourist destination and do all the tourist things, host fun events, and see live music. All on my terms and while striving to offer others a better quality of life at the same time. Who could ask for more?

— **CHARLICE ARNOLD**
  email: hello@charlicearnold.com
  phone: 619-246-2070

WHAT IF YOU COULD PROSPER WHILE PLAYING WITH YOUR PET?

By Amelia A. Johnson

I believe that if I do what I love to do and what my gut tells me will serve my purpose here, the money will follow. There were periods when I worked for a paycheck instead of following my heart; those were not happy times. They were filled with long hours, little time for my pets, friends or family, and far too little appreciation for a job well done.

I love animals. Even as a little girl, I knew I wanted to work with animals. In 1971, I opened a dog grooming salon. I loved making dogs look and feel better. I retailed dog products for a network marketing company at a time when people were made to feel guilty about spending money on their dogs. After all, they were just dogs, not members of the family as they are now. Many years later, I sold the business. The relationship with the network marketing company that had recruited me to sell their grooming products also ended.

I then followed my heart to apprentice as a horse trainer. Unfortunately, I was not happy as an employee working long hours with limited income and dealing with horse-related injuries that required hospital treatment. After satisfying my goal of developing world-champion horses for amateur riders, I once again moved on to a new challenge.

Pet sitting had now become recognized as a profession, so I started a pet sitting and dog training business. In 2002, a network marketing representative for a pet product business sent me a postcard. It just so happened that I was looking for better products for my own dog, so I followed up on the offer for a sample of their dog food.

The company was still in its infancy, and I was skeptical on many levels. I knew the public was not being told the truth about the quality of pet food at that time. However, my senior dog chose to eat this company's products rather than a dozen other high-quality foods that he had tested. I trusted his judgement. That's when I decided to go into this business with my dog.

I met with the company founders, owners, and staff before fully committing to offering their products to my clients. I discovered that the company had and continues to have the same core values that I do when it comes to serving our pets so that they can live longer, healthier, and happier lives.

As the company has grown and prospered, so have I. This company is privately owned, so I know it will be here for the long haul. As representatives, we help make decisions for new, functional products. The compensation plan is simple. This company that I am with is in it for the love of pets. That's why I am proud to be representing them.

In all my previous businesses, I could stay in my comfort zone as an introvert because people sought out my services. I succeeded through satisfying clients who referred business to me. I don't consider myself a salesperson, but I know that I can satisfy my clients with the products that I offer for their pets just as I did with my previous services and so now, I am successful with this, too.

As I was working my pet sitting and training business, I didn't have the time or the desire to go through the yellow pages or cold call other pet professionals that I didn't know to try to convince them to "work" the business with me. I was not comfortable in that role at all.

Twenty years ago, shopping online was only for the brave. There was a lot of resistance towards getting scheduled deliveries of pet products and then having to pay for shipping.

I knew in my heart, and I could see with my eyes, that the pets that were enjoying our products were happier and healthier. In turn, my teammates grew their businesses as they reached out to groomers, breeders, boarding kennels, pooper scoopers, dog trainers and veterinarians as well as the everyday pet owner.

I kept watching my commission check increase. Wow! I realized that my own dog products and veterinary care were being paid for by my commission check. I was getting very comfortable with this side hustle.

I closed my traditional business over a decade ago to care for my parents. Thankfully, what started out as a side hustle with network marketing now provides me with a healthy dependable and residual income. I am stretching my comfort zone as I learn how to attract customers and teammates to me through various social media strategies. These pet lovers that I meet ultimately say "yes" to the solutions that I can provide their pets as they get to know, like, and trust me.

I am having fun making new friends while making more of an impact on the improved health and happiness of pets. My heart sings because I am in alignment with my purpose of serving pet owners.

I see more possibilities now that so many people are accustomed to meeting one another and doing business online. I can use social media to meet with people that love animals the way I do. I can also work when and where I want to work.

This network marketing company is my home. It supports me in being who I want to be. It enables me to serve the people that I want to serve. It will keep me forever young.

Would you like to stay young with me? Say "yes" to yourself and your heart!

— **AMELIA A JOHNSON**
website: AmeliaAJohnson.com
email: Amelia@AmeliaAJohnson.com
phone: 301-539-2393

CHOOSING TO STAY IN

By Carla Archer

Awkward... is the only way to describe being a Tax Collector at a party. Either people walked away, had some ill words for my employer and what I did, or had a question about something going on with their Aunt Nelly's tax return. I often thought of making something up when people asked, "what do you do?" to avoid any of these responses.

Although I took great pride in being a public servant, I loved the investigative part of my job and I worked with amazing people. The problem was that every day, I was faced with fear and anxiety over who was going to unleash their wrath on me or who might show up on my doorstep. I knew that I held the position of authority, yet this did not offer me any sense of comfort nor satisfaction. It just was not me.

No one was ever happy to hear from me, and that was really difficult energetically, particularly in the end stages of my career when I was working with what I would describe as a very challenging clientele.

Most conversations were a result of an action that I took because the client had been avoiding me, and once I did get their attention, they were not happy. It generally resulting in being called choice words, confrontation, hanging up, them calling back, generally more upset, more choice words, no resolution, more action, and on and on it went.

I did my utmost to stay positive, appreciate the good job that I had, yet I found little joy in what I was doing for my livelihood.

Fortunately, I was working in the background on a plan for early retirement, and at the age of 39, I was able to say goodbye to the bad party conversation.

From the age of 17, I had wanted to be a Fitness Instructor. Twenty-two years later, I fulfilled that dream. I became a certified Fitness Instructor. I started my own company, and I began teaching fitness classes in my local area. I was able to spend time with positive people who were happy to see me. They sometimes still swore at me depending on how hard the workout was, however, they had a smile on their faces when they did. More so, I was doing what I was passionate about. Yet. it still felt like I had a greater purpose, that there was something more for me.

That was when I discovered my network marketing company through a friend of mine. She had instantly thought of me as a fitness instructor and all of the benefits I might find from the products. She was right!! I am so grateful that she reached out to me. I had incredible results with the product and when she told me about the business, I was very intrigued.

This product was so unique and in perfect alignment with who I am and for my clientele that I said yes to the opportunity. I just knew this was the right place for me, that THIS WAS IT!! What "it" was, I had no idea.

This is when I discovered a side of the business world I had never known before.

I witnessed people coming together with a common goal to change lives and to revolutionize our health care system. People who were happy to help a colleague with no financial ties. Who had purpose and passion for their work. Who were so comfortable in their own skin the thought of supporting someone else and helping them to rise to their fullest potential was met with great satisfaction rather than insecurity and the feeling of being threatened in their status or position. This space and place was safe for my self-discovery and personal growth all the while allowing me to just be myself. I knew this was it; this was a family, this was home.

My network marketing company has led me to other opportunities to learn and connect with some of the most amazing friends and mentors. They have taught and inspired me to build my network marketing business in a way that feels aligned with who I am.

Something changed for me to be able to come into alignment, and it all started with a choice of the language I used. Commonly, in our industry, we hear the expression "Get Out of Your Comfort Zone" and I will admit, not knowing there was another option, that I also used this language and taught this strategy. I quickly found out that I did not need to get out of my zone or my way to create success in my business. I learned that I was able to choose comfort with what I was already capable of which allowed me to take steps towards growing in those areas. This feels much better than being kicked out into the vastness of the unknown outside of my comfort zone with the expectation to figure things out.

This sense of being in true alignment with who I am has shown me that I have value and has given me the confidence to build the Brand of Me.

In doing so, I have been able to marry my two loves, fitness, and my network marketing product to support my very specified audience in a way unlike ever before. I feel it in my heart and my heart feels happy that I am choosing to work with an audience I not only love and adore, but I can also relate to because they are me. These are my people.

I stopped looking out of my comfort zone and started to look in my comfort zone. I connected with my heart and found what truly has felt authentic to be my audience to serve.

Am I a work in progress still? Absolutely.

Do I feel like I am exactly where I am supposed to be? 100% and I will continue stretching inside of my comfort zone every day as I continue to build.

— **CARLA ARCHER**, Launch Your Fit Biz
  website: launchyourfitbiz.com
  email: launchyourfitbiz@gmail.com

WHERE IS MY (DIS)COMFORT ZONE?

By Kathleen Mitchell

I've enjoyed various comfort zones in my life. I enjoyed a safe childhood to teenage years with normal angst in times of transition, such as junior high to high school, to college. I married, had a 30-year teaching career, raised two children into independent and self-sufficient adults and now in current seasons, I am in a second marriage became a caregiver for my sister-in-law and then for my mother.

Now, I've taken on my present role of Network Marketer. When I first signed up for a NWM business opportunity, I envisioned such grand dreams. The first was to be able to pay for my monthly auto-ship. Secondly, I wanted to give my husband the opportunity to retire when he chose. My upline sounded so confident saying, "Caring is sharing." My introduction into NWM's strategy to success was, "No boss, no set hours; time, location, and financial freedoms; just continually share with family and friends and in no time, you'll have oodles of income."

My comfort zone involved activities such as teaching, education, informational classes, and meeting people at restaurants and coffee houses. These were mostly family and friends who I hoped would buy something and declare its wonder-working power to their world. That worked for a while, till I could no longer in good conscience continue to approach people who were not ready to 'fix their lives' with my products. It was no longer comfortable to stop strangers at the grocery story, or post office if they appeared to be a likely candidate for my goods. It became downright UNcomfortable. So, my comfort zone was transitioned again.

What glorious timing to be introduced to a different way to find my people. To learn skills that would attract to me the people who actually need and want my goods and services. People that I can serve. Because of my own life experiences, I can speak into their lives and help them envision a more fulfilled life for themselves and their family. I will be living my dream by helping others live a better life. There's just one problem with this scenario. And in discovering this, I found myself in a unique position. The actions needed to create the reality of my dreams are not within my current small comfort zone.

Here's my good news: As a believer, I know God has a plan for my life. He has equipped me with everything I need to fulfill the plans and purposes He has for me. Extraordinary aspirations require extraordinary capabilities. Am I willing to learn and do them? Why not stay in my present comfort zone? Why should I try a new comfort zone? What does that even look like?

I heard a definition of comfort zone that applies to two areas: outward and inward. Outwardly, everything I am physically able to do, while inwardly, or inside, it feels easy, with no mental resistance. A popular example is driving a car. Following this line of thinking, outside of the comfort zone I would encounter mental resistance. If I choose not to push past the resistance, it gets harder to step out. It's in the stepping out and actually expanding the comfort zone where growth can occur. By growing myself, my comfort zone can continuously expand. Expand to meet me where I live the way I want but only if I'm willing. Then this new zone becomes natural and comfortable. If I disregard discomfort and don't let it have a say, my life will expand and be wonderful. As I expand my comfort zone, joy and peace move with me.

As the size of the bowl dictates the size of the fish, having a small comfort zone will keep us small. Though our dreams may be big, and in our hearts, we know God placed them within us, if we aren't willing to expand our comfort zone, on our death bed, I believe, will be regret. I, for one, and I already know there are many of us, want to leave as few regrets and as large a legacy as possible.

Order and predictability are comfortable, would you agree? It sounds like a great life, until one day you may realize you never really lived. The Bucket List remains in the notebook. The dreams remain unfulfilled in your head. If this is true, this idea affirms that growth only comes in times of disruption or discomfort or unpredictability. Here's the risky part. As entrepreneurs, we accept that order changes and things become unpredictable and risky. We select to change order. We accept the risk. We relish the growth that is anticipated to occur.

The quote, "Life begins at the edge of your comfort zone," could have the added tag. "It's not as scary as it looks." I have triggered the change myself. I know that an ordered environment is a threat to my realizing my dream/vision/future into reality. Order-disrupting people, I think of Jesus, have proven this. My growth, and thus finding fulfillment, are based on seeking discomfort. Seeking to find what's on the other side.

Some say life is a constant push against the comfort zone. Expanding our comfort zone, and thus our whole life, must lead to extraordinary days ahead. What if inside my comfort zone I find the fear of failure exists? What if I push my comfort zone out further? Might I find bravery and courage there? What if I accept the fear and do it anyway? My future resides in a brand spanking new comfort zone, a comfortable location because my core values live there. Virtues and ideals and beliefs that I will defend to the end. Values that empower me to seek the unpredictability of change, as occurs with growth.

As long as the growth promotes forward and constant movement, I will declare success is occurring! My efforts now are focused on becoming the person who can step into that future life and live comfortably, surrounded with joy and peace.

BIO: A professionally trained educator and classroom teacher turned network marketer, this is Kathleen's second literary contribution. She resides in Alabama with her husband, James, and their foxhound, Stanley, where she helps caregivers grow their home-based businesses online. Kathleen enjoys visiting her adult children in Huntsville and Denver.

— **KATHLEEN MITCHELL**
  email: jokats74@gmail.com

FAILING FORWARD

By Tracey Cook

I remember August 2016 just like it was yesterday. It was a sliding door moment that I never knew would change my life the way it has.

I was lying in bed, recovering from major surgery, after having cervical cancer. I remember my husband saying, "When do you think you'll be back at work?"

He meant this in the kindest way. But we had to be realistic also.

You see, I was a corporate manager, on my feet all day, in a stressful and high-performance based job role. The surgery and recovery were initially expected to take eight weeks recovery time. We could handle that financially and emotionally as a family. Yes, we could get through that.

Sometimes, life throws you curve balls, and I had extremely major complications; I felt anxious, scared and we didn't have a back up plan at all. Our savings were going down, the stress and worry going up, and I was feeling hopeless and at a loss for a solution.

Although we had very little money, I remember scrolling through my iPad and seeing a product that I thought might make me feel better, if only for a moment. I messaged the lady and she dropped it off the very next day. I was finally expecting and allowing some girlfriends to visit me. I wanted to look pretty. It was a lipstick product. I longed to feel womanly and pretty if only for a visit with my friends.

I got dressed up, put on my lipstick, and my friends were commenting on how good I looked. Being a natural sharer, I told them about the lipstick and how the most basic thing makes you feel like yourself in a time a self-healing.

Amazingly, they all asked for the woman's number to buy some. Again, being a natural sharer, I passed it on, and they also loved it. Weeks went by and my recovery was still slow. I had been made redundant from my position, and we were now at risk of losing our home.

It was in that darkest time that I took a call from the lipstick lady. She said, "You have been sending so many people my way, thank you, but I'm not sure if you know you can make money from this?"

I'll never forget those words. It was like a life raft had just been thrown to me at sea.

I had just been introduced to network marketing! I joined on the spot. We were literally down to our last couple of hundred dollars. Thoughts were going through my head of "What will my husband say? I don't know how to do this. Is this a scam?"

I had to make this work. I didn't have any other options with my recovery still months away. I got straight to work, had a home party, and grew a large team fast. I ranked fast and while I was not earning thousands, it was enough to keep food on the table and the bills paid. I was also making new friends. I felt like I had purpose again and it was fun. It literally saved my family.

As time went on, I went back to corporate and kept my side hustle. The best part about it, is that it still fills that gap on most months. The community is what keeps me involved. I get to expand, still stay in my comfort zone, and still feel the growth while I build on my own self-belief. The NWM community feeds my soul with support and this industry now gives my family another stream of income to see us through on those months that are sometimes harder than others. It's great being able to breathe and not be scared of opening a bill again.

Fast forward to 2021 with the internet, social media, and entrepreneurship. Home-based businesses are a growing industry and strongly related to lifestyle choices. I thank the universe daily for the self-development, trainings, networks that I encounter on every step of this journey, and it's all because I said YES!

I failed forward, made mistakes, embraced the opportunity and I'm blessed to share those experiences with other entrepreneurs with the power of YES!

— **TRACEY COOK**
  website: www.traceyleecook.com

I'M IN MY COMFORT ZONE – ARE YOU?

by Sigrid McNab

Your Comfort Zone—just what exactly is that?

The Oxford definition says that it is a place or situation where one feels safe or at ease and without stress. Okay, that sounds good. So why do people constantly tell us that we must get out of our comfort zones to be successful?

Why is not being out of our comfort zone so frowned upon? And why is it assumed that if you're not pursuing this notion of a comfort zone that you are not doing things correctly?

What about staying in a place where you feel comfortable— where it's possible to interact with others and act like yourself while earning a really good living?

Is there such a place?

You betcha! It's found in Network Marketing.

Network Marketing allows me to be my authentic self and be in alignment with my core values. It makes it possible for me to stay where I feel comfortable. Where I feel safe and secure. Less anxious and stressed. And still make a good income.

So, what does it mean for me, personally, to be in my comfort zone?

I'm living and acting in alignment with my most authentic and positive self. I get to create my perfect day, every day.

I have the freedom to put my family's needs first. Every time.

I can be the mom my daughter and son need and be there for my daughter 24/7 as the caregiver she requires.

My schedule is flexible and allows me to spend time on the things that are important to me - family, friends, fun, and my self-care.

Being out in nature is crucial for me. It makes me feel grounded, peaceful, and calm. Gazing at the blue ocean, hearing waves crashing, smelling the salt air, and digging my bare feet into the sand makes me happy.

Walking through a cool green forest, smelling the dirt and moss, hugging a tree or being in my daughter's flower garden where the air smells so sweet and pure - now that's a great way to get grounded in my opinion.

Being with my daughter when she goes to the barn to ride her horse so we can spend special one-on-one time together — that's part of my comfort zone too.

I'm able to do all these things when I want and where I want, and work at that location at the same time. If I want to.

What would it mean to you to be in your own safe comfort zone and still be successful and earn a good income?

Do you have obligations at home? Children or sick parents?

Do you have a boss that you have to plead with to get a couple of hours off to take your child to a medical appointment? To plead with to get your vacation at the same time your kids are off school so that you can spend quality time with your whole family together at the same time?

Just this past week, as a family, we looked at the weather report for the coming four-day weekend and decided immediately not IF we could go camping, but WHERE we would go. I did not have to ask my boss or plan my yearly two-week vacation months in advance to have time off from the job.

We're able to travel almost every weekend to visit family, friends, go to places we've never been, or just simply get away at a moment's notice. And again, work along the way—if I want to.

I love being able to tell my daughter that we're taking this weekend off to go walk on the beach. I'll catch up with my work when we get back.

I'm a bit of an introvert. Sometimes I just don't want to go out and talk to people in person. So, I don't.

Network Marketing has given me independence, financial freedom, more time with my family, my choice of working location, and the lifestyle I choose.

It has given me the freedom to be me and that makes me happy. I have gained confidence, increased my skills, and enhanced my life with love.

It won't be constant "golden" moments in this lifestyle all the time. However, I feel it's important to shine your own light, be one with yourself, and grab life with both hands and live it fully.

How about you?

You might not have control over many things, but one of the things you do have control over are your choices. You, and only you, get to determine what you want to work on. Don't do things that you know will not benefit you just because someone else says you need to get out of your comfort zone.

Move out of your comfort zone for something you really care about, not because external influences or peers make you feel that you should. Or because you're trying to prove to other people that you can do something.

Staying in your comfort zone allows you to be yourself and listen to your intuition.

Staying in your comfort zone doesn't mean being stagnant; you can still try new things and evolve. When you feel safe and secure about who you are and what you want to do, it can actually be easier to learn new skills while staying in alignment with who you are.

Don't ditch yourself and your authentic values by wishing to be someone else just because they say that you should. Forget what everyone else has or is doing. Ask yourself: "Does this give me the freedom to be me and genuinely make me happy?" If not, do what feels best for you.

I wish you much happiness, love, and success in your life. I care about you even if I haven't met you yet. If you want to learn more about my specific company that is in alignment with my core values, or if I can help you in any way, please contact me directly. I'd love to get to know you.

— **SIGRID MCNAB**
  email: sigridmcnab@gmail.com
  phone: 250-954-8416
  website: www.sigridmcnab.com/downloads
  facebook: www.facebook.com/McNabSigrid

BEFORE I KNEW WHAT FREEDOM REALLY WAS

By Tiffani White

I spent 25 years working for "the man." The last 15 were spent teaching middle school science in the public-school classroom. I have worked in fast food, retail, and full-service restaurants while earning my degree, surviving on student loan after student loan. I got my Master's in 2018 with the anticipation of becoming a professor to develop future educators. Teaching is my truest passion.

Time is our most expensive commodity, and now because of network marketing I get to spend my time independently however I choose. This allows me to spend more time with family and I can work from anywhere in the world at any time. I do not have to wait until retirement at 65+ years old, instead I got to start at age 39. That is 26 extra years of not being confined to a desk in a classroom restricted to political hierarchy and constant ridicule for having too many opinions or ideas, defending my sexuality, or religious beliefs. (Yes. Exercising religion out loud is frowned upon.) I am no longer strapped to a chain of command typically without a growth mindset, trying tirelessly to beat a system that is broken, amongst other tireless, seemingly effortless responsibilities. Been there, done that, burned that t-shirt.

We only get about five defining moments in our entire lifetime, moments that change our destiny. These moments never seem to come at a stable time, rather they always come in the messiest of times. The miracle happens in the mess, my friends. If you are not self-employed, I encourage you to step forward in faith instead of backwards in fear. Start living the life and the freedoms you have always dreamt of. In my very small opinion money is not what necessarily makes you rich, time does. There are three C's in life: choice, chance, change. You must make the choice, to take the chance, if you want anything in life to change.

The biggest change in my life since stepping forward in faith and becoming self-employed is the time freedom. I had my business established for three years before the pandemic hit in March of 2020. I just used it as a very fun, creative outlet to earn extra money for frivolous spending and travel. I had no idea it would become the bane of my existence in the fall of 2020 and essentially save my life from one of the most severe depressions I have ever experienced. Without those friendships specifically formed through network marketing, zoom calls, late-night brainstorming sessions, how to pivot our businesses in a tech-savvy manner, zoom happy hours, competing with dozens of friends around the nation, crunching some of the biggest numbers we have ever seen amongst so many other new breaking points, I am terrified to think of where I would be today. Returning to the classroom was not an option for me that fall, the pandemic was a catalyst in that decision. I thought I would teach until the day I died. It turns out God does know what he is doing after all. We may make our own plans; however, God has a master plan.

You may wonder what I mean by time freedom, so let me elaborate for you how my work days vary depending on how life is going. This week, I did not have to ask anyone for permission or days off to head to New Orleans from Thursday through the following Tuesday to help my baby sister wedding venue shop, an impromptu girls' week. I can run my business from my phone which means I can work as little or as much as I'd like from anywhere, in the whole world! That means my office is anywhere on any day or night that I choose. So, where is your office today? I also make it a steadfast rule to put together 10 sample packs, connect with 10 new people and collect their information while I am out of town. That way, I will have tapped into a brand-new cold market for my upcoming monthly virtual event. Anyone from anywhere can attend, one of those pivot brainstorming sessions we had during the beginning of quarantine led to an idea that has now become a crucial piece of my monthly business operation.

Two more values that have been able to surface and quickly became the bane of my existence are individualistic expression and a newfound belief in myself through personal development. Let me explain. As an educator (in certain conservative parts of Texas anyway), you are expected to remain conservative and conform to a certain lifestyle. I like to call it in the closet if you will. My hair must be a certain natural color, my tattoos must be strategically placed as to be covered by regular clothing. I cannot express my individuality too loudly. I am not a radical person by any means, but I will never forget such a small, simple right that was "taken" from me just a few short years ago. Today I can do these things without asking a single soul. In the beauty industry, it is very on trend to have bright fun hair colors, small peas, I know. I am talking mermaid, rainbow, turquoise—I know you have seen all the beauty influencers with it! Boy, did I want my platinum blonde hair to go rainbow as soon as June 1st hit for the summer and posted my upcoming look on Facebook. Within 30 minutes, my principal at the time, was standing at my desk telling me I would not be having rainbow hair that summer. Her exact words were, "If you showed up to a doctor's office and your doctor came in with hair like that, what would your thoughts about her be? Let's keep it professional." And that was that, no fun rainbow hair for me that summer or at all. Blonde it stayed; no individuality for me. No fun self-expression in this conservative place or career path. Which I had always been fine and well with until I found myself in network marketing and right smack in the middle of the beauty industry.

Now let's talk about that newfound belief in myself through personal development. The last 15 years I had only focused on personal development by way of developing my teaching craft, becoming the best possible teacher I could and phenomenal at teaching I became. Network marketing self-development is different though. Who knew I was not only a leader in the education world but a leader amongst empowering other women at harnessing their own self-esteem and growing during times of weakness and teaching them how to love themselves as Christ sees them? Something I have not been allowed to do in the education world, another in the closet topic—religion. The world of network marketing focuses on a whole new world of personal development, topics I have deprived myself of my entire adult life. This is no one's fault; I just was not around people who talked about these kinds of topics on the regular. You can't know what you don't know, right? Topics such as the power of focus, growth mindset, the art of vision, communication skills, personality styles and their triggers, harnessing your power with a morning routine, dominating at leadership, and the list goes on and on. I now want a second masters. I want my MBA. I never had an interest in marketing and business when I was younger. I come from a long line of entrepreneurs who tried to talk me into that career field. I was not interested, but now that I have tapped into it, have been shown my abilities and someone took time to foster and coach me to have faith in myself, I cannot get enough.

If you tried network marketing and failed, I urge you to try it again. Perhaps the timing, the season or the company was not right. If you have never tried it and are curious, I encourage you to try it out and make sure you get under someone who is a phenomenal coach and works their business consistently. One week I may hustle hard for three days, working 14-hour days, then coast the rest of the week on auto pilot and take it easy on a ghost hunting trip to Boston with my best friend. The point is, this career path is my life on my terms and I command my salary. This month's effort determines next month's harvest. I have never felt this kind of freedom and I don't plan on turning back anytime soon. I am so blessed to be able to teach, coach, and train women in this field in which I accidentally ended up in at 35 years of age. Everything I have experienced has prepped me for this season, this career, this moment. After all, teaching is my greatest passion. The difference is, now I do it on my terms and I can get more than a 3% annual raise. How crazy bananas cool is that?!

— **TIFFANI WHITE**, M. Ed.
email: Tiffani.White81@gmail.com
phone: 325-671-6986

EMBRACING THE EXQUISITE RISK OF UNCERTAINTY

By Rebecca Reilly

The joy and freedom I am now experiencing had been locked in a vault and I just recently discovered that I always had the code to unlock it.

In grade school, I remember the thrill of being in the front of the class presenting a project or report. As I became a teenage girl, I internalized the societal message that I was too much and at the same time, not enough. I learned to conform and be on the outside of the party.

In my early 30s, I started my own cooking school and catering business. I loved teaching. I loved engaging with people and sharing my passion. It was a mixture of theater and art for me. Whether I was in front of small gatherings, an audience of hundreds or in front of the TV cameras, I felt alive, and my world finally made sense! I saw so much possibility.

Years later, I no longer desired being the star and decided that a steady paycheck, no matter how meager, would fix all my problems. External family pressures to "Get a real job" had worn me down! It was like going from the frying pan into the fire! I was unaware how this decision sacrificed my core values of nurturing, compassion and giving service to others. I traded my time and values for dollars and the approval of others.

My children and I paid a high price for that decision. Taking on the employee mentality was not becoming on me. In the end, trading my talents and expertise for far less than I was worth was demoralizing. I became a slave for that weekly paycheck. It was at this time that I realized a traditional job and I were like oil and water; we did not mix. I felt like I was psychically drowning.

I knew starting a brick-and-mortar business again was not my calling either. A friend of mine had her own private business as a companion at nursing homes and had started referring clients to me. I also began cooking meals for a woman in her 80s who became a very special friend. Word of mouth spread, and I was back to being my own boss, this time with no overhead.

My friends and I became the "lunch bunch" at one of the nursing homes. We would gather with our clients for lunch or take them out on nice days to enjoy the fresh air. It was like having a party filled with conversation and laughter. I even gave cooking demonstrations, sharing my love of food. The residents looked forward to the live cooking show, the amazing smells, and of course, the tasting. After all, who doesn't love cooking shows? It took a while before my attendees felt comfortable sharing their food memories.

Being a compassionate elder companion, as we jokingly call it "is a dying business" and not for everyone. The human connection was so fulfilling. However, one by one, our clients passed away, and then came Covid! By this time, I had already admitted the work was unsustainable for a multitude of reasons. The emotional toll was wearing me down. The compassion I so deeply felt for my clients was now turning into resentment. There would never be financial freedom in my future if I didn't make changes.

Before Covid, I was introduced to Network Marketing. The first company sounded like a perfect fit and a way to financial success. Unfortunately, the sales method they taught left me feeling inauthentic. Several years later, I was approached to join another company. The products were about wellness. This time, one of my uplines started doing boot camp coaching for us. As difficult as it was to wrap my head around the technology and Network Marketing on Facebook, I loved the group training and the deep personal connections I was making. I was determined to free myself from the robbing Peter to pay Paul lifestyle I was leading. The idea that I could work from home and build a legacy excited me.

On March 17, 2020, on my 69th birthday, life as we knew it changed for me and millions of others worldwide. In a perverse way, the pandemic shutdown was an opening for me to make the changes I had been talking about. I had reconciled myself to the daily grind of working seven days a week and feeling like a hamster in a cage. Running on the wheel going nowhere was unsustainable. I welcomed this timely uncertainty the world was entering.

When my phone rang on the morning of March 31st, another major life opportunity was presented to me. My sister was ready to leave the hospital to continue her stroke recovery at home. The only requirement was she must have 24/7 care. I had been a caregiver/ companion for other families' loved ones for 12 years. Without realizing it, I had been training for this day. The next morning, I packed a small suitcase, grabbed my cat, and my computer and headed off to Portland, Maine to bring my sister home.

I couldn't believe my luck. I could be a loving sister, while working on building my budding online business and never leaving the house. I no longer needed to fit in the online training at night when I was completely exhausted, nor would I be too tired to cook healthy food for myself. I could now take a break to cook something wonderful for me and healing for my sister while rediscovering the kitchen as my comfort zone.

During that year from April 2020 to April 2021, I immersed myself in the world of Network Marketing. I had always been comfortable being in front of any size group and on camera for TV. Social media marketing was different somehow. I did not have the knowledge or the computer skills like the way I did with food and cooking. Fortunately, there was a ton of training available. My team introduced me to several different successful leaders, all with very different coaching, teaching, and marketing styles. Finding what fit for me was not easy because nothing felt authentic to me. It wasn't long until I was not having fun. It felt like I was trading one grind for another.

Then, in April 2021, two things happened: the "Go For YES"™ marketing training program created by Stacey Hall attracted my attention and someone shared with me how they healed a similar health issue to mine. This led me to another Network Marketing company. Instantly, I knew in my core that I wanted this to be my home. The associations I made and the coaching and training I received since saying "Yes," are giving me the freedom to incorporate my passion for sharing, healing, teaching and being onstage, while also building financial security.

The most priceless reward for my recent choices is the knowledge that I will be available for the birth of my first grandson. The second reward is I will have the freedom to visit my son where he will be stationed and begin his career as a JAG officer. No vacation time will be used, no permission will be needed and there will be no loss of pay!

A bonus with all that freedom is that my sales are growing and will continue to even when I'm spending time with my family and friends all because I said "YES" to Network Marketing.

By saying "no" to the unsustainable grind, I have reclaimed my ability to play, explore, and discover in my own time and on my own terms.

— **REBECCA REILLY**
email: rebecca.rreillygf@gmail.com

FREE TO BE ME IN MY COMFORT ZONE

By Rachel Rideout

When I sat down and thought about what about how Network Marketing helps me stay in my comfort zone, it didn't take me long to find my answer. I absolutely love how Network Marketing helps me be more creative! In fact, it has helped bring back my creativity. For a long time, I felt that I had lost my "mojo." You see, when I was younger, I was a writer. I wrote songs and poetry. But as an adult, I felt like I lost that part of myself.

When I am home, in my comfort zone, and not boggled down by the stresses of a job, my mind can be free. I am free to explore, learn and grow personally and professionally. The more I explore and learn, it not only helps me, but in return, I can help other people. It is such an amazing feeling to be an inspiration to others and help bring back the passion and creativity they may have lost.

Network Marketing has helped me become more confident in myself and my abilities. I don't have to be like anyone or everyone. I am free to be me and in return, I will attract the right people to me. Being able to stay in my comfort zone of what I allow into my business and what I am a part of is such a comforting feeling. Network Marketing allows you to have choices, unlike a job where you do not get a say so in your daily activities or how you choose to work your job, where someone is always telling you what to do and how to do it. You are truly free to be you and stay in your comfort zone, if that is what you choose to do.

I would like to add that staying in your comfort zone is great, but that you should not be afraid to also step out the box a little. There is nothing wrong with testing the waters, even within your comfort level, but pushing past it just ever so slightly. Sometimes you must get a little uncomfortable to be more comfortable later. Take chances and if it doesn't work, you can always go back to what is comfortable to you. Life isn't fun without a little risk involved! You never know what could or could not happen if you don't step out your comfort zone every once in a while. Listen to your gut; it usually won't steer you wrong.

One more important piece of how Network Marketing helps me to stay in my comfort zone is knowing that I can help my immediate family. Being able to bring in income that helps financially brings a sense of peace to my mind. It allows me to pay for my grandson's extracurricular activities and other unexpected expenses. When you know you have a way to help your family and loved ones, it is such a feeling of satisfaction. Being home daily with the ones you love the most definitely puts you in a place of comfort.

— **RACHEL RIDEOUT**
website: www.rideout2success.com
email: Rideout2success@gmail.com

BALANCING LIFE FROM THE HEART

By Sunita S. Pandit

Network Marketing (NM)– a business model that offers me an atmosphere for conducting business from my heart. As the wife and practice manager of a cardiologist, I have learned many medical things related to our hearts. With the challenge of caring for not one but three family members in my life, I have strategically navigated balancing work and home.

God has blessed me with two sons. My oldest, Sachin, was born in November of 1981, 10 weeks early. He was labeled as a 'special needs' child with a diagnosis of severe cerebral palsy and mental retardation. I walked away from a promising career with IBM as several attempts at finding proper caregivers left me frustrated. In the U.S., I am one of those that has left full-time work to care for a special needs child or aging parents, creating a loss of income that averages $18k a year. (I left more than that!)

Network Marketing to the rescue? For me it is a blessing from God! As a computer science major, I am overly analytical, making me a physician's nightmare as I question everything and do not stop until I fully understand and have a plan of action. With my non-verbal child, I had to become the 'ultimate physician's nightmare,' so he would never have to suffer in silence for any reason. Network Marketing companies offer a plethora of products in a variety of categories that enhance our lives. I have explored over 20 companies in order to find a few 'body friendly' solutions for my son. In this journey, I have been able to care for all my family and myself, with great results.

Sachin's first occupational therapist offered me some serious sage advice—she said, "Please do not put your child in a gilded cage… treat him as normal as possible!" I concluded the only way to succeed was to be strategic about it above and beyond the norm. This was the beginning of my system that I can proudly call Strategic

Caregiving. I always follow a simple rule — 'Put yourself in that person's place and think about what you would want or need so you do not have to ask but can anticipate their needs and get it done!'

As a result, I have successfully avoided the dreaded surgical knife for my son. Many products from a variety of Network Marketing companies synergistically blend together to give me satisfaction that I am doing the best I can within my human limitations. I am not able to be super mom as I have many responsibilities. The reason I can honestly say that 80% of the products I have chosen for my son are from Network Marketing companies is because of the wonderful one-on-one interaction the marketing system has in place. I could learn from a practical and practicing view of how to implement usage of products for my son. Some worked wonderfully, some had no effect, some worked for a short time, and the prize few are his saviors.

Because I cannot commit to eight hours of work outside the home, the Network Marketing model works beautifully for me. Even the work I do for my husband is mostly from home. I have a choice and I must choose wisely to create a harmonious atmosphere for myself and family. The versatility of working in my 'cracks of time' in the Network Marketing model is a blessing. Many companies do not have proper training on this, but I figured it out. Like all successful endeavors, this also needs structure and discipline. And wonderfully, it spills over into caregiving, so the recipients of my care are humming like a well-oiled machine! I do get high praise from my mom, and my dad (a PhD in Geography) granted me a PhD in Life! I sacrificed not only my career at IBM but also a master's degree in computer science.

At four decades of caregiving, I look back on my life experience knowing that God only gave me life lessons and guided me into choices to prepare me for this future I live in today and beyond. I am not after pushing people into the world of Network Marketing. I am definitely on track to educate those that seek knowledge so that they can effectively come on the path needed to reach their personal goals. My experience shows for me to pray for the correct outcome, not the money.

— **SUNITA S. PANDIT**
  email: sunita@strategiccaregiver.com
  website: www.strategiccaregiver.com

WORKING IN MY PURPLE ROBE

By Koriani Baptist

I rolled my eyes, thinking to myself like, really!? How am I supposed to track down that many people!? I felt awkward and apprehensive just thinking about how these conversations would play out. Would these people even remember me, much less BUY from me!??!

"$13.00 per appointment." That is what my college boyfriend kept telling me.

Working full-time and going to school full-time, the sound of making a few appointments and getting $13 bucks for each was enticing.

So, there I was sitting in this small room with about 50 other college-age students for orientation. We were told to write down a list of a hundred people to talk to about knives. We were instructed to think of everyone in our life, starting with family, then to elementary school friends, and keep going until we reached 100 names to contact.

I wrote my family's names down, including my mom and even some of her friends and neighbors. I only had 45 people. None of my current friends had their own place, and if they did, they weren't going to spend their little money on cutlery.

I am a loyal person and wanted this gig to really work out.

However, after months of calling that contact list and getting stood up, I was beginning to feel like a failure. I did manage to get a few appointment meetings and even enrollments. However, after five long months, these conversations with family and neighbors that felt forced, and I quit. Looking back, I am glad I had this first network marketing training experience.

I know how it felt to be told to do something, and even though I felt awkward, and uncomfortable, yet I still complied.

The feeling of being out of alignment is something I never want to experience again. I now train other Network Marketers to stay in their Comfort Zone.

What I took away from this experience was that I really liked the idea of making money by helping people. Also, being able to set my schedule by booking the appointments around my college classes.

To this day, I still use those wonderful knives in my home. Looking back, I could have totally lumped all network marketing companies into this first experience and judged the whole industry.

However, I am grateful that I have learned a more comfortable and satisfying way of being in network marketing. Those days of staring down at a blank sheet of paper, trying to remember somebody's name, to hound to buy anything I sell, are OVER!!!

After graduating from college, my life seemed to be "on track." I had my own place, and I was working full-time. On the weekends, I would paint, and I even started selling my pieces at local vendor shows and events. It was at one of these events where I found my Network Marketing Home (NMH). Do you know that feeling when you get Home and there is Joy, and Calm? I equate my NMH to my absolute favorite article of clothing, my robe.

My robe is SO soft, the perfect deep purple, has a hood, and it even has pockets! I have such joy in my robe. It brings my whole body into calm and is so comfortable. I never want to take it off!!

I even keep my favorite network marketing products in the pockets to help me and my kiddos stay above the wellness line. Another perk of being able to run a business from a laptop or my phone is being in my robe while I help others get wellness tools for themselves and their family.

Similarly, in my NMH, I know the products, I trust the products, I am truly in full alignment when teaching or talking about the products, and/or the business opportunity. By using social media, my team is full of people who were once strangers, but now are dear friends.

This is why I don't need to make a list of my family and friends. I don't have to hound and beg people to buy something just because they are related to me or are my friends. It's such a freeing and empowering feeling of relief to use attraction marketing to grow my team and stay in my comfort zone.

The friendship and relationships I have with my essential oil team, upline, and crossline are so infused with joy, trust, love, compassion, and loyalty. There have been seasons in these past six years when I thought that doing this business was not for me. There was frustration and anxiety. I am not proud of those moments, and yet I know that everything really does happen for a reason.

When I can stay true to my calling, stay in true connection with my God-Given Purpose, there will be results and sales. Sales comes easier when I stay anchored to my purpose. My purpose is to help stressed out women find and keep calm so they can fulfill their God-Given purpose with simplicity and ease.

Being a match to those who want to hear and buy what I offer, is so satisfying and brings such light and joy to my life. These results are the stories I have in my heart of healing myself and my children. Seeing and listening to testimonials of a life transformation is so inspiring. Where someone doesn't have to wait for weeks to get a second opinion from a doctor, they can lean into their own intuition and listen to their gut! If any moments of self-doubt do arise, any team member could go to tons of product education Facebook groups, including the one I lead, to get validation and encouragement of which oil to use for any occasion.

I adore the company I represent and am proud to be a part of a movement of people who want wellness for themselves, their family, and community. As I write this wearing my purple robe, this is MY freedom, connection, and COMPLETE comfort.

Priceless.

— **KORIANI BAPTIST**
  email: blessingkeepers@gmail.com

MAMA BEAR AND HER CUB

by Monique Christine

Roughly two months before giving birth to my son, I came to the quick and painful realization that I would be a single mother. It didn't take long for terror to set in. Here I was, nearly 28 years old, with a child on the way and no clue how I would provide for him. The only thing that I knew was that I was madly in love with my baby boy and that I would do everything in my power to keep him safe.

As a child, I experienced several traumas that I refused to have my son repeat. I knew that I needed to work from home to feel like I was doing my job as his sole protector and provider.

So, I enrolled in my local university for its online Medical Billing & Coding Certificate program. Not only could I study online, but I'd also be able to find work-from-home positions. But I'll be honest. I was NOT passionate about entering codes for health conditions into electronic health records.

But what did passion have to do with responsibility? That was my thinking until a dear friend offered me an opportunity to combine my love for a healthy lifestyle with earning income from anywhere in the world.

I was all in, but there was a problem. I had no clue how to market my new business opportunity and quickly burned through my list of family and friends, only to discover that I felt like I was living a lie. It now felt like I had become a sleazy car salesperson convincing people that they needed the shakes and supplements I was offering to be healthy, despite their ridiculously high cost.

If that weren't enough, the company's business model left me no real options to make the business my own but instead to model what every other distributor was doing, which did not feel authentic. Less than one year in, I decided to leave the company behind, but the promise of being my boss had forged a fire in my belly, and I could not ignore it.

I knew that working for myself was the only option, but I needed to make it work for ME. So, I switched my major in college to Complementary & Alternative Health to support the direction I yearned to go. Instead of "forcing" my audience to believe that they needed scientifically engineered shakes and supplements, I wanted to offer them a wealth of knowledge along with natural solutions to fit their needs.

I realized that there was no shortage of companies with products to offer. All I had to do was have a solid foundation of holistic wellness under my belt to feel comfortable and confident enough to truly help my future clients. I began to study marketing and finally shifted from a notorious spammer to a bonafide health and wellness professional sharing value and solutions, mixed with an empathetic heart to genuinely care for the wellbeing of those I would soon help.

With the three pieces of the puzzle in place, I was now free to do what I love from the comfort of my own home while keeping my son safe. And boy, oh boy, am I glad that I trusted myself.

I had no clue that we'd soon be dealing with a global pandemic that would change everything about life as we knew it. But in my corner of the world, not much had changed. My son was already going to school online, and I grew my business virtually, so we didn't have that many adjustments to make.

Suddenly, my work-from-home plan was brilliant and ahead of its time. I went from feeling entirely invisible in the online space to becoming a great asset to new entrepreneurs who needed to create job security that the pandemic had taken from them. Not only was I able to help people grow their businesses from the comfort and safety of their own homes, but my expertise in holistic wellness grew in demand, seemingly overnight.

With a world looking for ways to stay healthy from home, it became abundantly clear that I had unknowingly created job security for myself as well by simply following my gut. That little voice that whispers so quietly you've got to still yourself to hear it. Yes, that voice led me to the promised land before I knew what it was.

All I knew was that I had a desire to keep my sweet boy safe from trauma as much as possible and to be present with him instead of leaving him memories of spending most of his time with his grandmother or another caregiver.

Network marketing has allowed me to create new, lasting friendships while deepening the connection with myself and finally showing up as my full, authentic self without feeling constrained by a typical 9-5 job.

I work my business around my life instead of asking a boss for permission to live my life. I am my boss.

Network Marketing has given me time to face and heal my traumas, prioritize my health, and share my gifts with an unlimited number of souls searching for solutions. This beautiful profession allows me to stand in my power, use my talents for good and healing while keeping my son safe. I even teach him to think like an entrepreneur instead of preparing him to work for someone else to make their dreams a reality. Network Marketing has altered the course of our lives by giving us the means to dream and reverse-engineer a plan to turn those dreams into our reality.

Network Marketing isn't rocket science, nor is it a walk in the park. It takes time, focus, and dedication to make it work. But I can promise you that if you work it, it will be beyond worth it. I wanted to be free, and Network Marketing was the ticket to get me there!

— **MONIQUE CHRISTINE**
email: support@moniquechristine.com
website: www.glowupwithmc.com

UNSCRIPTED UNLIMITED

By M. Susan Patterson

Thank goodness for being sick. Well, honestly, being sick wasn't really a pleasant experience; at the same time, I'm guessing it was the metaphorical 2x4 God used to snap me out of my rut. Through illness, I found my next life's purpose, a way to help others and a means to make my life what I wanted it to be.

Illness brought surgery and medications into my life; it also brought an introduction to organic, natural products that changed the way I viewed wellness and opened up a whole new world. These products empowered me to find joy, energy, calm, and strength. I was skeptical, as you might expect, when I was introduced to these products. And then, Divine Intervention intervened.

After leaving public education, I decided to enter the world of online work. At first, I assumed that would be teaching. After multiple attempts at several online education jobs, I discovered that it was the same old thing, living by nonsensical rules, making very little money, and not really helping anyone at all. I wanted to be my own boss, and, very importantly, live by my values, my beliefs, and my rules. Helping others improve their lives was vital, as I was no longer willing to tolerate operating outside my comfort zone, that is, according to someone else's value system or rules, following a script, or teaching like a robot. Although it took me awhile to make the connection between my personal success with health and wellness products and the selling of these products, when I finally did make that connection, it was a life-changing decision. I just didn't really know what I was doing at first.

When I first began network marketing, I was told to do and say certain things, have a class, give samples, share information, and success would magically appear at my doorstep. Well, that wasn't exactly how it happened. In fact, the scripted, step-by-step sales pitch didn't work at all. The best response I ever got was a polite, uninterested stare that pointedly indicated it was time to stop talking. Logically, how could a scripted, generic pitch work for someone looking for real answers anyway? I blamed myself and thought, what have I done wrong? Maybe I'm not enthusiastic enough, maybe I didn't give away enough samples, maybe, maybe, maybe …

The truth is, I didn't do anything wrong – I was just following inappropriate advice. People don't respond to a scripted speech, and they certainly do not want a generic, pat answer. For a very long time (it seemed like forever to me) I searched for something different. I wanted and needed some way to really connect with people. Why? Because I had a product that had helped me immensely, a product that helped me to feel better physically, emotionally, mentally, and spiritually, and I wanted to share it. This had become a mission for me, much more than just a way to earn extra cash.

Through a series of coincidences (do you believe in coincidences? I don't either) I asked a trusted mentor about marketing in a way that made sense to me, that felt true to my values. He immediately knew what I was looking for, it really was kind of uncanny. (Unless, of course, you believe that the Divine is always present.) He suggested I contact a particular Success Strategist, Stacey Hall. (Yes, the Stacey Hall who is publishing this book.)

My life began to change, I learned that teaching and selling according to my values and my rules was okay. In fact, helping people, being genuine, living what I taught, all these things were part of the "Go For YES"™ marketing training program created by Stacey Hall. Over time, I learned that there are basically two approaches to sales. One is the corporate clone style where every member of the sales team looks the same, sounds the same, and speaks from the same script. This method is what I call "The Negative Approach." It doesn't work for me. The second process is what Stacey calls the "Go For YES"™ Formula. When I began to learn about this, church bells rang, the sun came out, children laughed, and the angels sang. Okay, seriously, it was a big deal for me. The reason it was such a big deal was because I could speak to my clients and prospects with sincerity and truth while still addressing their individual needs and wants. This was my comfort zone: living what I professed, helping people with their distinct problems, and guiding them to their appropriate personal solution.

This was a huge revelation – I could be compassionate, kind, gentle, and helpful. This is who I am, not the corporate version of me. In the Go For YES Masterclass™ Coaching Group, I found myself with a large group of people who wanted to live, work, and sell like I did; in other words, marketing with compassion, seeing the needs of others and helping them resolve their issues. I realized this was a lot bigger than me; each one of us had a vision of changing our corner of the world. Here was a movement, a way to change the world for the better. This would genuinely make a difference, and I wanted to be part of it.

Wait, there's more! In the process of my giant "Change the World" epiphany, I discovered that people do actually want honest, clean, organic products that will help improve their lives. I now had the ability to guide them to a better way, a better product, a better life. For me personally, this felt like what I'd been looking for. I could make a living helping others and live according to my values, my rules, and my approach. Why does this matter so much? Because the standard corporate, industrial-age mind set simply does not work anymore. People want something that works for them individually, not a "package" that works for the generic public. And that is precisely what I can deliver. No more trying to fit a square peg into a round hole! That's beyond exciting! Through this new framework, I discovered that it was okay to be me, that it was a good thing to talk to people as individuals, that I could treat people with true respect. What does this mean to me? It means my world is unlimited. Think of all those platitudes that you've heard, free-to-be-me, the-world-is-your-oyster, if-you-can-dream-it-you-can-achieve-it, etc. That's my world now. Really.

My opportunities are boundless, I am my own person with my own approach, true to my beliefs and values. The "Go For YES"™ Formula not only allows me to understand my client's problems, it encourages me to examine their challenges and offer solutions. This philosophy promotes the idea that I can listen to my client sincerely. I can take the time to understand their problem, and I can explain to them how they can find solutions. It is a viewpoint that is genuine, from the heart, and truly helps people, all while allowing me to live in a way that is deeply satisfying and successful.

Now, you may wonder, why share all this? If I can have such a fulfilling, prosperous, and effective life, why shouldn't you? I want you to know that your impact, your voice, and your mission in life matters. You will make a difference in your corner of the world, and you will be astonished at how happy you will be as you make that difference. You and the work you were meant to do is important, it counts, and the life you were meant to live is waiting for you to claim it. So, reach out and grab hold. It'll be the best thing you ever did, for you, for those you care about, and indeed, for the world.

— M. SUSAN PATTERSON
   phone: 603-593-8816
   email: edge.patt@gmail.com
   facebook: https://www.facebook.com/sudiebleu/
   website: http://edgelifevision.godaddysites.com

RELEASING THE PAST

By Kathy Joy

Most of my life I have known mental, physical, and sexual abuse. Sadly, it became the norm as it does for many.

I got pregnant at 15, married at 16 and divorced at 25. I rented an apartment and thought I was free of all the shame and guilt that I had been carrying around my entire life. However, I still felt like I didn't belong and was unworthy of anything good.

Eventually I met someone who pampered me and made me feel good about myself. It was such a huge difference. After a few months, I moved in with him thinking I was worthy and finally belonged somewhere. It didn't take long for the physical and mental abuse to begin all over again. It seemed as if a magnet drew this type of person to my life and I couldn't understand why.

I stayed with my partner for almost 30 years. Then, one day it suddenly hit me like a ton of bricks that this was no way to live. I had to do better!

So, I made a list of all my bills and started working a lot of overtime to pay them off. I looked at houses on weekends to see what I thought I could afford. I began cleaning out everything where I was living and preparing for my big move. My partner thought I wouldn't move out, but I kept my head down and worked.

In 2009, I found the perfect house in a great school district. I had saved enough for a down payment, so I signed the papers. I drove to the new location on weekends and watched our house being built. However, the fear of not being good enough rose up again big time! I tried get out of the contract, but to no avail. I remember crying as I fearfully signed the final papers.

Moving day came and it was stressful! All the thoughts of inadequacy came rushing up. I cried believing I was making a huge mistake. However, I loved having a house to call my own! My mindset shifted from "I have", to "I get" to! Such a great feeling!

After a few years, I began to struggle to make ends meet and realized that I needed to make more money. I searched online and found the work-at-home industry. I joined an MLM and went to work thinking it was the answer to my prayers. It wasn't. Even though I loved the products, I couldn't do some of the things they were asking me to do. You know, like make a list of 100 people and go after them until they signed up. "Call them until they were dead!" is what I was taught. It didn't feel right to me. My heart and stomach were sick all the time and I couldn't do it. I wanted to make more money by help others, but not by pressuring them.

I found someone in a company and loved the way she presented herself. We became friends and I began to follow her. When she left the company and went somewhere else, I went with her. The second company was better, and I did make a little money, but again… spamming people was just not in my heart and soul. I didn't like doing business that way. I wanted to get to know people and genuinely help them help themselves.

In 2017, my mom got very sick and passed the next year. We learned two weeks before she passed that she had stage 4 cancer and it was too late to do anything. My life was rocked again. She was my best friend. I went into a deep depression and laid in bed for days and cried. One day I just couldn't stop crying and I reached out to my friend. She got me to agree to seek help. I wound up getting medicated and going to counseling. My counselor was great. She seemed to totally get where I was struggling. We worked a lot on my mindset and how to shift from "why" to "thank you for the time and great memories." After each appointment, my mindset shifted, and I felt a little better.

At age 61, I started going back over the conversations I had with my momma while she laid in the hospital bed. She talked a lot about her past. I never knew some of the things she went through until then. She was German and lived through WWII. Her life was a living hell having to forage for food, sometimes go hungry, live in the woods and watch her back every minute. It got me to thinking about my dad. He grew up with 12 brothers and sisters in a 3-room shack with a basement and an outhouse. He quit school in 8th grade to help the family out. When he was 17, he joined the Army and would send money back to his parents to help them out. He always worked so hard for everything.

Pieces of the puzzle were beginning to come together. I realized that it wasn't me that was at fault, and it wasn't my parents' fault. They raised me the only way they knew how. I began to see them in a different light, was able to shift my mindset, and start letting go of the guilt, shame, and hurt. It no longer served me.

Through extensive mindset work, I was able to release and forgive others that had hurt me. Some of which are now my friends.

I finally understood that my life has purpose! Serving others is the path to fulfilling that purpose. It took a lot of mindset training and work to learn that I have a lot of value to share.

My mission is to teach others how to shift their mindset to overcome their past and live in the present, so they can focus on the future. I did it, and I know others can do it as well!

— **KATHY JOY**
email: kkjoy@aol.com

GOING FROM STRENGTH-TO-STRENGTH LIVING IN MY COMFORT ZONE

by Karen Bromberg

Even as a child I never wanted the run-of-the-mill kind of job I saw everyone else have. I didn't want to be beholden to a boss. I didn't want the 9-5 grind. As a teen, I longed to be free. I wanted to be able to listen to my inner voice and muse.

Maybe it was what I saw at home. On my days off from school, I'd watch my parents getting ready for work. My father, an outside salesman, made his own schedule so sometimes he'd be out the door by 8 a.m., other times he could lounge around until 11.

Each evening he'd regale my mother and I with stories about how he'd march unnoticed into whatever secretarial pool of whatever company was on his list back then, in a voice that was meant to disrupt, and say "Well . . . here I am!" He'd set up his wares in the middle of the room, then offer the secretaries a cup of coffee or bouillon. This, of course, was years before Mr. Coffee and the Keurig.

The women would sip, and my father would go into his spiel. Next, he'd meet with the bosses. More often than not, he'd make the sale. One would think he'd be happy, but he never looked to be. He'd complain about the quotas his boss imposed on him and what would happen if he didn't meet them.

My mother, by contrast, had to be up, out the door and on the express bus to Manhattan by 7:45 a.m. so that she could have enough time to buy her morning brew, punch in and be at her desk by 9. She'd drag herself back up our block in the evening, simply exhausted. I'd see her from the top of our stoop and run to meet her. She'd complain all the way into the house, "I can't even go to the bathroom without him bellowing for me," referring to her boss. It was nothing I ever wanted.

It would be decades before I'd learn what my core values are and what it meant to live from my comfort zone. By the time I graduated with my B.A., I knew I wanted to be of service and to make a difference. My uncle – my father's brother – was making a difference. He was a podiatrist with his own practice. Each time my parents and I would visit him in his office, I'd watch him with his patients. The way he'd smile while working on their corns, conversing with them as if they were old friends, inspired me. While my parents were in service to their bosses, my uncle was in service to people.

I decided to become an audiologist. It seemed to fit me best. Doing that meant I could have my own practice and, like my uncle, have meaningful relationships with those seeking my skills. The added benefit was that I could have what my uncle had and not have to have someone's feet in my face. The latter was big deal for me.

My plan was to love my career the way my uncle loved his, and I couldn't wait for the day that I could finally graduate and begin working. What I didn't realize, though, was that the only way I was ever going to have my own practice was to spend at least $100,000 just on equipment. That was on top of my student loans.

The only option open for me was to work in someone else's practice. Most times, I'd work in an M.D.'s office. That meant all the relationships I'd hoped to establish had to go through that doctor. What's more, if the doctor wanted a day off, I had to have the day off too (often without pay) and if he/she wanted to make up that time by working late the following day, I had to as well.

The hardest part was acknowledging that I was nothing more than the M.D.'s appendage. That was not what I went to school for. By this time, I'd already been in the audiology field for several years. I felt choiceless. I felt helpless. I didn't know what else to do so I tried to make the best of it.

My turning point came shortly after my parents passed. On a phone call with a friend, she began telling me about the products she'd recently started selling. The more she spoke, the more hooked I became. When she told me about the business opportunity, I knew I was home.

What I wanted, no, deserved, was more money, more respect, and more time to do the things that were important to me. I was tired of serving at the pleasure of whomever was in charge. If he/she didn't like something I said or did, I could lose my job.

A weight lifted from me when I teamed up with my buddy. It was the first time I didn't feel like I had to sell my soul to make a living. I also didn't feel like I had to kiss someone's ring to get, then keep, a job or twist myself into whatever pretzel I had to in order to make it all okay.

At last, I had choices. At last, I was free. It was the first time I'd ever felt that way.

Since then, that sense has only grown because what I've discovered is the joy of living in my comfort zone and being aligned with my core values. What power . . . such peace . . . all born out of strength.

I now look forward to each day, stretching the boundaries of my comfort zone, growing in joy, growing in confidence, going from strength-to-strength, and finally, paving my way to my future.

— **KAREN BROMBERG**
website: karenbromberg.com
email: karen@karenbromberg.com
phone: 347-644-9209

CREATE A TEAM OF BUSINESS BUILDERS, NOT JUST CUSTOMERS

by Ron Wilder

As a rookie distributor, my main issue was primarily cash flow. Already $100K in credit card debt with no solution to the problem, my wife, Liz, was enduring a full-time job she was not enjoying, and I was attempting to develop an online business. We had invested heavily in learning online marketing, but it hadn't become profitable yet. I was earning merely hundreds of dollars per month and, to add insult to injury, there was a good chance that Liz might be laid off right before she could retire! We were really in a pinch! Since she was still at work, it was up to me to figure out something fast.

I had joined our MLM company to help a friend (sound familiar?) with no intent to build it. Curiously, I received a $22.45 check from our company, and I didn't know why. After I figured it out that a friend had bought some products without me even knowing about it, I realized this was the easiest money I'd made in a long time.

Considering my various opportunities to create cash flow, it came down to let's try this one out and see where it goes. I planned to give my MLM business a month to see where it might go, and when I asked my sponsor if I could make $2K next month, she said, "Sure!"

So, our journey began. My sponsor shared with me her method of their process, but I felt uneasy doing it her way. I did not know how or even if the products even worked! They were very "woo-woo," and I was a licensed professional electrical engineer, not a woo-woo kind of guy.

So, like the engineer I am, I studied the company's compensation plan to determine how to maximize my profits in the least amount of time.

I discovered something interesting: the thousands of dollars a month I was hoping to generate by selling products wasn't practical. I had to sell $10,000 a month, EVERY MONTH, just to earn $2000 a month. That's a lot of work!

However, by studying the comp plan, I also realized that the big bonuses came from the product flow within a properly structured network of people who bought their own products and/or sold them.

This was an "A HA!" moment for me. I just had to figure out how to create the proper business structure to generate the cash flow I required.

I immediately got to work learning how to add people to our team without the worry of creating a bunch of salespeople.

I discovered it was actually easier to prospect for people who wanted to change their lives than to learn all about the products.

I started asking simple questions like, "Would you like to make this year the best ever? What would that look like for you?" I would then ask more questions to dig a little deeper. Questions like, "How much do you think that would cost?" and "When would you like to achieve this?"

I would then follow up with something like, "I love your goal for the year! In case you weren't aware, I am building a business where I help people attain their goals, and I'd be thrilled to work with you at no charge if that would interest you."

The cool thing was that I could teach this to everyone who joined, and I wouldn't have to learn, teach, and sell all the products.

Ultimately, I pursued my more comfortable "people-centered" approach to grow my business. In just over a month, we earned a couple of thousand dollars a month of income. Three months later, Lizzy left her job and decided to not get another one. A year later, we were "Diamonds" in our business.

How? We had built a team of business builders, not just customers. That was over 10 years ago.

Today, we have the time and resources to do things that really matter to us. For myself, it is writing books like *Beyond the Products* that help network marketers think differently and creating online MLM training platforms like the MLM Mastery Club that connects network marketers with MLM experts of all types.

For Lizzy, it is helping spouses become effective support partners in their MLM businesses while keeping their relationships harmonious.

From our beginning to the present, I stayed within my "comfort zone" of leveraging the products to start conversations focusing on guiding people to build their dreams and I'm SOOO happy I did. They are too!

So, what do you want to do with the time you'll have when you hit your business goals? How will you stay in the "comfort zone" of personal integrity to get there?

Keep smiling,

Ron

— **RON WILDER**
email: Ron@MLMMasteryClub.com
website: www.MLMMasteryClub.com
website: www.BeyondTheProducts.com

EPILOGUE

By Stacey Hall

I have had the goal to produce this book for many years.

Having written two #1 best-selling books previously, it was important to me to make it possible for others to express their voice, make a difference and leave a legacy that will live on long after they are gone.

With this *Power of YES* book series, I feel I have achieved my goal in a soul-satisfying way.

Throughout my career, as successful as it is, there were many times I would have picked up a book like this to receive encouragement and a reminder to keep my eye on what is truly important... especially on those days that were less-than-wonderful.

Each of the Authors you have met in this book are people I respect deeply for how they generously serve so many people through their business.

And, in addition to these Authors, I have many more people to acknowledge for their support and encouragement in bringing this book series into reality.

First and foremost, I acknowledge and appreciate the support and constant guidance I receive from God, the Divine Creator, the Gracious, the Powerful, the Generous, and the Loving!

Next, my appreciation and love goes to my husband, Bill, who has been my partner in every way that I could ever want a Partner to be.

My respect and admiration to Lil Barcaski and her team at GWN Publishing for also being just as committed to publishing and distributing this beautiful and enlightening book as I am!

My ever-lasting gratitude goes out to the founders, staff, coaches, and members of My Lead System Pro. There are thousands associated with this organization that deserve to be mentioned by name. And because of space constrictions, thanks for understanding that I am specifically mentioning Brian Fanale, Todd Schlomer, Norbert Orlewicz, James Fanale, Melanie Lozano, Rhonda Reiter, Troy Boyd, JP Letnick, Jimmy Ybarra, Anthony Jackson and Joe Tarin, who made it possible for me to know all the others!!

The endorsements for this book make my heart smile each time I read them. Thank you to (in alphabetical order) Erin Birch, Haylee Crowley, Russ DeVan, Mark Harbert, George Madiou, Jim Packard, Tara Rayburn, Jackie Sharpe, Antonio Thompson, Jerry Yerke and Dr. Joe Vitale.

My appreciation extends to and surrounds everyone I have ever attracted into my life – my family, friends, clients, coaches, teachers, publishers of my previous books, my upline sponsors, my team members, business and cross-line brainstorming partners, those who help me care for my health and well-being, and the network marketing companies, whose products I and the Authors in this book have been blessed to represent.

Special recognition goes out to my pups – Lucy and Francesca (known as 'Frankie') for all the walks we missed and the reduction in cuddle time while I was producing this book. I am putting on my walking shoes now and getting your leashes. *Let's go.*

My appreciation extends to each reader of these words.

To learn more about the "Go For YES" sales success formula mentioned throughout this book, reach out to the Authors or visit book.goforyeschallenge.com.

You will discover:

A 4-step plan to authentically sell more of your products in a way that makes you (and them) feel amazing.

How to identify your audience's pain points so you can speak to their soul and influence them to take action.

The source for never-ending content ideas and daily strategy for what to post and when for maximum results.

Where to establish your social media presence to connect with your audience when they are ready to buy.

And you will find satisfaction and a successful way to make more sales and serve more people.

I would love to hear from you.

Send your endorsements, comments and questions to me at stacey@staceyhallonline.com

"When I think of genuine heartfelt leadership, I think of Stacey Hall. She is an incredible trainer in the profession of Network Marketing. She has a proven track record helping people get results using her "Go For YES" formula. Devour every bit of wisdom she has gathered here. You will NOT be disappointed!"

— **MARK HARBERT**, Marketing Expert & Trainer
MarkHarbert.com

BUSINESS STRATEGY & DEVELOPMENT

Once we find the pain points, hone the messaging, and get clarity for you and your business, our team brings the goods!

LONGBARCREATIVES.COM | 727-348-6682

GHOSTWRITERSNETWORK.COM

Ghostwriting
Editing
Coaching
Publishing
Writers Retreats
Book Marketing

GFADDESIGN.COM

Branding | Logos
Graphic Design
Web Design
Printing
Promotional Products
SMM Management

Proudly Published by

GWN PUBLISHING

A DIVISION OF LONGBAR CREATIVE SOLUTIONS, INC.

GWNPUBLISHING.COM

CPSIA information can be obtained
at www.ICGtesting.com
Printed in the USA
JSHW031802190222
23006JS00004B/27